INTRODUCTION

Have you ever wanted to understand more about music, or write your own?

Part 1 of *The Little Book Of Music Theory and Musical Terms* will give you an introduction to the language of music and help you understand its essential simplicity. So if you have ever been curious about how music works, this is the book for you. The concepts explained here are common to all Western music, be it classical or pop, rock or folk, blues or soul. If you've ever wanted to write your own music, an understanding of these fundamental concepts will help.

Once, only writers on classical music talked about musical theory. Now, increasingly, books on popular music are using some of its ideas and terms. Whether you're a singer or an instrumentalist, a member of a string quartet or a rock band, or just someone who loves listening to music, knowing a little theory will enhance your awareness and increase the pleasure music gives you.

Part 2 of this book is an invaluable A–Z mini music dictionary containing all the definitions you need for both classical and contemporary music styles.

The Little Book of

Music Theory

and Musical Terms

Published by:
Wise Publications
8/9 Frith Street, London W1D 3JB, England.

Exclusive distributors:
Music Sales Limited
Distribution Centre, Newmarket Road, Bury St. Edmunds, Suffolk IP33 3YB, England.
Music Sales Pty Limited
120 Rothschild Avenue Rosebery, NSW 2018, Australia.

Order No. AM977053
ISBN 1-84449-019-x
This book © Copyright 2003 by Wise Publications

Book design and music processing by Digital Music Art.
Cover design by Chloë Alexander.

Printed in the United Kingdom by Printwise (Haverhill) Limited, Suffolk.

Your Guarantee of Quality
As publishers, we strive to produce every book to the highest commercial standards.
Particular care has been given to specifying acid-free, neutral sized paper
made from pulps which have not been elemental chlorine bleached. This pulp is from farmed
sustainable forests and was produced with special regard for the environment.
Throughout, the printing and binding have been planned to ensure a sturdy, attractive
publication which should give years of enjoyment. If your copy fails to meet our high standards,
please inform us and we will gladly replace it.

www.musicsales.com

Wise Publications

London / New York / Paris / Sydney / Copenhagen / Berlin / Madrid / Tokyo

Part 1. Music Theory 5

Part 1.
Music Theory

1. THE BASICS

Centuries ago, long before the invention of any recording technology, people played and created music. They needed a way of preserving it and teaching it to other musicians. The question was, how? The answer: invent a diagram.

The Stave

The result was the stave, five lines where notes are placed on or between the lines, lower or higher according to their pitch.

Stave

The Treble Clef

To fix the pitch of the lines, we use a clef (from the French, meaning 'key'). The treble clef is a squiggly shape beginning on the second line of the stave. This fixes the position of that line, as the note G. The treble clef is also sometimes known as the G clef.

Treble Clef

Letter Names

There are seven note letter names in music: ABCDEFG. There is nothing magical about letter names; any convenient shorthand symbol could have been used, including numbers. These are the so-called 'white notes' of the keyboard, and the sequence ABCDEFG is repeated over and over, from low notes to high.

The lines of the treble clef stave mark the notes E G B D F. Here's an easy way to remember this - think of the phrase Every Good Boy Deserves Fun. The spaces within the stave spell the word FACE. The space immediately below the stave is D and the space above is G.

Different Clefs

It is possible to have other clefs which change the meaning of the stave's lines. Apart from the treble clef the most common is the bass or F clef. This is most commonly used for the left hand of a piano part, and low-pitched instruments such as bass guitar.

The clef starts on the fourth line up, fixing the position of the note F. The lines now spell out G B D F A, the spaces A C E G.

Ledger Lines

If we need notes higher or lower than this we can use what are called *leger* lines. These are little lines which can be placed above or below the stave, for notes whose pitch is too high or low for the stave.

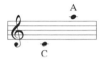

Several leger lines can be attached to a note, but obviously the more you use the harder it is for the eye to take in at a glance exactly how many there are. So if a piece of music involves a long succession of high ledger notes the symbol '8va' can be placed above the stave and the notes written one octave lower then they sound. This removes the leger lines and makes the music easier to read.

Transposing Instruments

Certain instruments are by convention not written at exactly the pitch at which they sound. This is because their range, written at the strict pitch, would take them too much above or below a stave. This would mean often using ledger lines and a headache for the musician! Such instruments are called transposing instruments. The notes they play actually sound at a different pitch than the same note played by a non-transposing instrument (such as a piano). Music for these instruments is usually written in a transposed key.

Middle C

The term Middle C is commonly used by musicians as a reference point. Middle C is the C nearest the middle of the piano keyboard. The frequency of middle C is often quoted as 256Hz (this is convenient for mathematical purposes) but the correct frequency at concert pitch (where A=440Hz) is in fact 261.62 Hz.

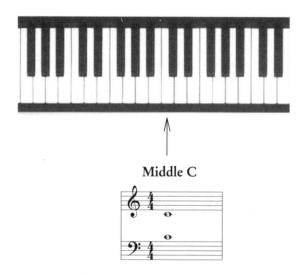

Middle C

Middle C is written on the first ledger line below the treble clef or on the first ledger line above the bass clef. This is still the same note but the treble and bass clefs are separated in order to make notes easier to read, and to distinguish between the left and right hands on the keyboard.

The music for many instruments can be written on one clef – the piano is an exception because it has a very wide range of notes from low to high. Consequently, its music needs a bass clef (for the left hand) and a treble clef (for the right hand). The two staves are joined by a bracket (see below).

Tablature

In recent years another type of diagram has been popularised for the guitar, which looks like this:

The six lines represent the actual strings of the guitar, unlike the stave which is a symbolic representation. Tablature, or TAB as it is abbreviated, is not a modern invention – in fact a similar form was used as far back as the 16th Century, for instruments such as the lute.

Instead of writing notes on the lines, fret numbers are written, so that the player sees immediately which fret to play on which string. This takes out one step in the reading process. With a conventional stave the player has to recognise what note is required, then decide where to play it. The disadvantage of tablature is that it does not give an indication of rhythm, so usually it is combined with a traditional stave to give a fuller picture of the music.

Unlike the piano, stringed instruments such as the guitar usually allow you to play the same note in more than one place. A player can choose where to play the note, and which fingering to use.

Here is an example of tablature for the bass guitar:

... and guitar tablature combined with the stave.

Here's a handy reference guide to some of the most common notations in TAB:

THE MUSICAL STAVE shows pitches and rhythms and is divided by lines into bars. Pitches are named after the first seven letters of the alphabet.

TABLATURE graphically represents the guitar fingerboard. Each horizontal line represents a string, and each number represents a fret.

4th string, 2nd fret — 1st & 2nd strings open, played together — open D chord

SEMI-TONE BEND: Strike the note and bend up a semi-tone (1/2 step).

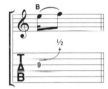

WHOLE-TONE BEND: Strike the note and bend up a whole-tone (whole step).

GRACE NOTE BEND: Strike the note and bend as indicated. Play the first note as quickly as possible.

QUARTER-TONE BEND: Strike the note and bend up a 1/4 step.

HAMMER-ON: Strike the first (lower) note with one finger, then sound the higher note (on the same string) with another finger by fretting it without picking.

PULL-OFF: Place both fingers on the notes to be sounded. Strike the first note and without picking, pull the finger off to sound the second (lower) note.

BEND & RELEASE: Strike the note and bend up as indicated, then release back to the original note.

LEGATO SLIDE (GLISS): Strike the first note and then slide the same fret-hand finger up or down to the second note. The second note is not struck.

SHIFT SLIDE (GLISS & RESTRIKE): Same as legato slide, except the second note is struck.

2.   ACCIDENTALS

Introduction To Intervals

Between any note and another note there must be an interval or a gap. In music there is a simple system for measuring this.

The smallest interval used in most Western music is called a semitone. This is the interval between two adjacent notes on a piano keyboard, regardless of whether they are black or white. As we have seen, the white notes of the keyboard are named A to G; most pairs of adjacent white notes (except B-C and E-F) have a black note between them. We can think of the black note between, for example, A and B as an A raised by a semitone (A sharp) or a B lowered by a semitone (B flat).

Sharps, Flats and Naturals

A sharp sign (♯) raises the pitch of any note by a semitone. A flat sign (♭) lowers the pitch of any note by a semitone. So A♯ and B♭ are the same note on the piano and are played by the same black key.

These signs are called accidentals. There is a further sign called a *natural* (♮) which cancels out the effect of a sharp or a flat. In rare instances a note is sometimes raised or lowered by a whole tone. This can result in a *double sharp* (✗) or a *double flat* (♭♭). Thus A✗ is actually the same note as B, but it may be necessary to preserve the rule that every letter must be present in a scale or key.

By introducing the five sharp/flat notes (sometimes called black notes) to our original seven we produce a sequence that looks like this:

A   A♯/B♭   B   C   C♯/D♭   D   D♯/E♭   E   F   F♯/G♭   G   G♯/A♭

Amazingly, all of our music is created out of just these 12 notes!

C   C♯   D♭   D   D♯   E♭   E   F   F♯   G♭   G   G♯   A♭   A   A♯   B♭   B   C

Octaves

There are several instances of each note name on the keyboard. For instance, the note A occurs eight times on a full-sized piano. These A's are at different pitches, but sound similar because their frequencies are related. Going up an octave (to the next occurrence of a given note name) doubles the frequency, going down halves it.

The best way to understand this is to locate several different instances, or octaves, of one note (eg. A), and play them, listening for the differences between them.

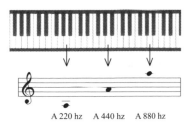

A 220 hz   A 440 hz   A 880 hz

3. RHYTHM

So far we've established how to represent the pitch of a note. But how do we indicate how long it should last, and what speed to play it?

Every note in a melody lasts a certain length - it has duration and rhythm. To represent this each note has a certain symbol, which is placed on the stave in relation to the other notes around it, at the appropriate pitch. This then tells us everything we need to know about the length of the note.

Here's a quick-reference guide to each note:

Symbol	Name	US equivalent	no. of beats
o	semibreve	whole-note	4
♩	minim	half-note	2
♩	crotchet	quarter-note	1
♪	quaver	eighth-note	$1/2$
♬	semiquaver	sixteenth-note	$1/4$
♬	demisemiquaver	thirty-second-note	$1/8$
♬	hemidemi-semiquaver	sixty-fourth-note	$1/16$

Here's what the notes look like placed on a stave. Tails can go up or down depending on various conventions such as which line they are placed on (notes above the middle line tend to have their tails drawn downward) or how many parts are represented at once on a single stave.

More complicated rhythms

Rhythms can be more complicated than we could notate using just these symbols. To be able to represent other rhythms and note lengths we need a few more symbols.

Dots

A dot placed after a note increases the duration of that note by 50%. Dots can only be used within a bar; they do not span bars. Here are some examples.

Ties

A tie joins two notes together. Only the first note is played, the duration of the second one is added on to the first (see below). This enables a note to last for more than one bar, or several beats plus a fraction of a beat. Dotted notes can also be tied to each other.

Rest

A rest is an indication of silence. This could be for part of a beat, a beat, a whole bar or many bars at a stretch. Each note has its own type of rest. Here they are in matched pairs.

Dotted Rest

A rest can also have a dot placed with it which adds 50% silence to the original length of silence. Here's an example:

1½ beat rest

Beams

As with the stave, certain conventions about the way music is printed have been created to make things easier for the eye. When there are a number of quavers or semiquavers in a bar they are usually grouped together, using 'beams' to make them easier to read.

Have a look at this example:

Here it is again written out in groups:

It's much easier to see the rhythm patterns now that the notes are grouped.

It is important to remember that musical notation - both rhythm and pitch - is to some extent approximate. The subtleties of pitch and timing in a singer's voice cannot always be exactly put down on paper, and the more precise a system of notation is, the harder it is to read. Standard musical notation is a good compromise between the extremes of simplicity and precision.

Tempo

In past times the speed (tempo) of a piece of music was indicated by Italian terms such as 'largo', 'moderato', 'andante', 'allegro' and so on. The interpretation of such terms as 'slowly', 'moderately' or 'lively' is to a certain degree subjective. A more precise method can be found at the start of most recent sheet music. You'll find a note, usually a crotchet (signifying the note value of the beat) and a number:

$$\text{♩} = \textbf{120}$$

This is the tempo expressed in beats per minute ('bpm'). A metronome or drum machine set to this tempo will give the exact intended speed of the music.

Time Signature

Whatever the tempo, and whatever the rhythm patterns found in each bar, almost all music has a constant beat. When you dance to music or tap your foot or drum your fingers on a table, you're responding to the beat. This is governed by the time signature - a way of organising the overall rhythm of the music. The note symbols given in the table above are given specific meaning by the tempo of the music and the time signature itself. On their own they don't really mean anything.

A time signature is found at the beginning of a piece of music. It consists of two numbers, like this:

Common Time

The top number refers to the number of beats in the bar, and the bottom number indicates which type of note makes up the beat. The most common time-signature is $\frac{4}{4}$, which basically means there are 4 crotchet, or quarter-note, beats in each bar. This is written in two ways (C standing for 'common time'):

Example:

How Many Notes In A Bar?

A bar of $\frac{4}{4}$ can use any number or mixture of notes and rests provided that the total number of notes and/or rests equals four crotchet beats.

The following example shows that many different patterns of notes can add up to four beats.

21

The following two bars show examples of too many beats in a each bar. These bars are impossible in $\frac{4}{4}$ time.

Simple Time

Other time signatures include $\frac{3}{4}$ (waltz time), $\frac{2}{4}$, and, less commonly, time signatures that use a minim, or half-note, as the beat, such as $\frac{4}{2}$, $\frac{3}{2}$ or $\frac{2}{2}$.

Occasionally you'll find bars of $\frac{6}{4}$, or even the asymmetrical $\frac{5}{4}$ (as in Dave Brubeck's popular jazz classic 'Take Five').

All of these time signatures are known as 'simple time', as each beat in the bar, crotchet, or minim, can be subdivided into two or four.

Compound Time

Fortunately, this doesn't mean time spent in prison! As well as having time-signatures which can be divided into two, there are also time signatures based on dotted notes where the beat divides into three.

⅜ is one such time-signature. There are six eighth notes (quavers) in a bar, however, they are grouped into two pairs of three, making a substantial difference to the sound of the bar, and the emphasis on the beat. Compare it with ¾ which has the same number of quavers (six) but three audible beats, since the quavers are grouped into three pairs of two.

Here's an example of ⅜ . The first bar shows the characteristic two groups of three quavers.

The first bar of this example of ¾ time demonstrates the difference in quaver groupings between ¾ and ⅜ (above).

Let's compare ⁴⁄ and ¹²⁄₈. Both have four beats. In ⁴⁄ there are eight quavers, but in ¹²⁄₈ there are twelve, grouped into four groups of three. ⁸ has three beats each of which divide into three. Compound time signatures such as these have a distinctive rhythm or 'bounce'.

Unusual Time Signatures

It is also possible to have odd-numbered signatures such as $\frac{5}{8}$, $\frac{7}{8}$, or $\frac{11}{8}$. These can be disconcerting because they tend to sound like $\frac{6}{8}$, $\frac{4}{4}$ or $\frac{12}{8}$ - but with one quaver missing. The rhythmic consequence of this foreshortening is that the beginning of the next bar always comes half a beat earlier than you initially anticipate - a factor which keeps audiences and performers on their toes!

Triplets

It is also possible to split a beat in simple time into three. This is called a triplet. Half-, quarter-, eighth- or sixteenth-notes can all be turned into triplets in this way. The triplet allows for a temporary change of rhythm which doesn't continue long enough to need a change of time signature.

4.   MAJOR KEYS

The basis of almost all music is a scale of some kind. A scale is a sequence of notes relating to a key, with a fixed pattern of gaps between each note.

The most important scale in Western music is the major scale. It is a way of dividing an octave into seven notes. Its pattern is made up of: tone - tone - semitone - tone - tone - tone - semitone.

Here's what happens if we start on C:

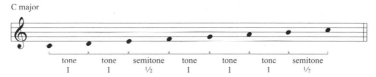

The gaps happen to be exactly where we need them and the two semitone gaps are in the right place – so there are no sharps or flats needed to make this scale fit the pattern of tones/ semitones. It can be played entirely on the white notes of the keyboard.

If we try the same thing on G something different occurs:

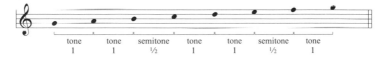

The first semitone is in the right place, but the second isn't - it has fallen between notes 6 and 7, instead of between 7 and 8. We have to make an adjustment, which is to sharpen the F to F♯. This makes the semitone between notes 6 and 7 increase to a tone, and also halves the gap between 7 and 8 - which is what we need:

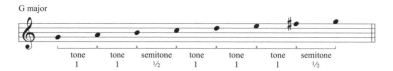

When a musician plays in the key of G major all the Fs are played sharp.

Now let's try starting on an F:

Now we have the opposite problem: the final semitone gap is correct, but the earlier one which should be between 3 and 4 is in the wrong place - between 4 and 5. The gap between 3 and 4 is only supposed to be a semitone but here it's a tone. To make it smaller, we have to flatten the B to B♭:

This gives us the scale of F major.

When a musician plays in the key of F major all the B's are played flat. This raises the question – why not use a sharp like this:

We could do this - but conventionally, every letter name must be present in a scale. So here, instead of a B, there are two A's. That's why we have to call A♯ a B♭ and think of it as the fourth note flattened, not the third note sharpened.

The Sharp Major Keys

It is possible to build a major scale from any of the 12 notes. Every key signature uses either sharps or flats (with the exception of C major, which has neither). Harps and flats are never mixed in a key signature. Here are the major scales of the keys which use sharps, in sequence:

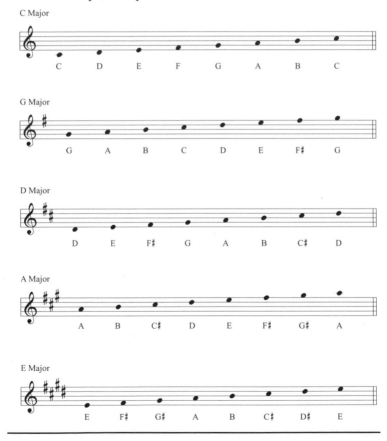

Here are a few tips to help you remember the progression of the sharp major scales.

> • The new additional sharp always appears on the 7th note.

> • All the sharps in a scale are carried over and automatically become part of the next until all the notes are sharpened.

> • The starting notes proceed by the interval of a fifth (see p37): C G D A E B F♯ C♯.

The key signature always appears at the start of a piece of music and tells you which sharps or flats to play throughout the piece (unless there are accidentals or key changes). The music would look very messy if the four sharps needed for E major were printed in every bar!

The Flat Major Keys

Here are the scales of the major keys which use flats, in sequence:

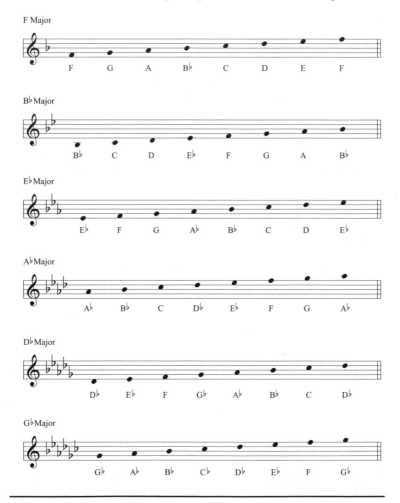

C♭ Major

C♭ D♭ E♭ F♭ G♭ A♭ B♭ C♭

Here are some tips on the flat major keys:

•The new additional flat always appears on the 4th note.

•All the flats in a scale are carried over and automatically become part of the next until all the notes are flattened.

•The starting notes proceed by an interval of a fourth: after C F B♭ E♭ A♭ D♭ G♭ C♭.

If there are only 12 notes, how is it that there are 15 major scales?

The answer is that three are actually the same, but have two different names: $D♭ = C♯$, $G♭ = F♯$, and $C♭ = B$. The reason for this is to simplify the notation and reading of a piece of music.

A piece of music can begin in one key, change to other keys, and perhaps finish in the original key. Changing key is called *modulation*. Key-changing is vital to most long pieces, avoiding monotony and creating the sense of a musical journey.

5.   MINOR KEYS

There are other ways of dividing up the octave. In contrast to major scales, minor scales have a sad quality to them. Whereas there is only one type of major scale (tone, tone, semitone, tone, tone, tone, semitone) there are three forms of minor scale.

The Harmonic Minor

The harmonic minor scale has an 'angular' sound, due to the different placement of the tones and semitones within it. Have a look at the scale below (A harmonic minor):

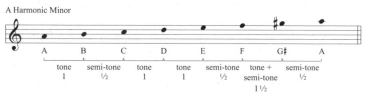

A Harmonic Minor

A	B	C	D	E	F	G♯	A
tone	semi-tone	tone	tone	semi-tone	tone +	semi-tone	
1	½	1	1	½	semi-tone	½	
					1 ½		

This scale is found more in classical music than in popular music, although rock guitarists sometimes use it when they want to produce an exotic, non-Western sound.

The Melodic Minor

The harmonic minor contains an interval (gap between notes) not present in the major scale - the augmented second, between the sixth and seventh steps. The melodic minor is a variation which smoothes out this gap, which can be awkward, especially for singers. Here's A melodic minor:

A Melodic Minor

A B C D E F♯ G♯ A G♮ F♮ E D C B A

The sixth and seventh steps of the melodic minor are both raised in the ascending scale, and both restored to their natural form (see below) in the descending scale. This makes it possible to write music in minor keys that avoids the angular sound of the harmonic minor scale.

The Natural Minor

The third type of minor scale is this:

A Melodic Minor

A B C D E F G A

This is called the natural minor scale. It is found in folk music, some classical music of the 19th and early 20th Centuries, and frequently in many types of popular music. It is also known as the Aeolian mode. We will talk about the scales known as modes a little later.

The Sharp Minor Keys

Each major key has a 'relative minor' which essentially shares the same key signature. The root note of this relative minor is always a minor third (1½ tones) below the major key root note. If you are using the natural minor scale, no additional accidentals will crop up in the music. If the harmonic minor scale is used, one additional accidental will appear in the music which would not be present in the major key. Here are the minor keys which add a sharp to the seventh note:

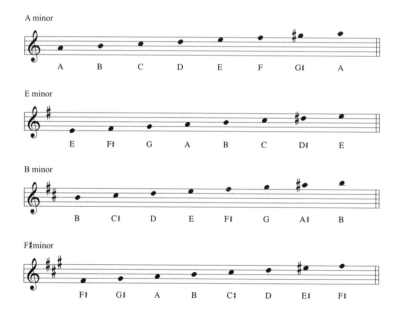

The Flat Minor Keys

Here are the scales of the minor keys with flats in the key signature:

The Flat Minor Keys (cont.)

Although these are flat keys, D minor and G minor use sharps for the seventh note, as it is an accidental (not part of the key signature), and also so that every note name can be represented.

6. INTERVALS

As we mentioned earlier (see Chapter 2), an interval is simply the distance between two notes.

The term *diatonic* refers to any interval occurring within the major scale. E.g: a major third = a distance of 2½ tones between the two notes.

If an interval is greater than an octave, it can be described as a ninth, tenth, eleventh etc. These are known as *compound* intervals.

Note that when intervals are turned upside-down they turn into the following:

minor 2nd	:	major 7th
major 2nd	:	minor 7th
minor 3rd	:	major 6th
major 3rd	:	minor 6th
perfect 4th	:	perfect 5th
augmented 4th	:	diminished 5th

Over the page is a diagram to measure the distance – or interval – between the notes within one octave. It is referenced against the scale of C, but to find these intervals in another key, simply count up (in tones/semitones) from the root note.

Interval Guide

Name of interval	Distance between notes (in tones)	Degree of scale (in C major)
unison	0	C - C *
minor 2nd	½	C - D$\flat$
major 2nd	1	C - D
augmented 2nd	1½	C - D$\sharp$
minor 3rd	1½	C - E$\flat$
major 3rd	2	C - E
perfect 4th	2½	C - F
augmented 4th	3	C - F$\sharp$
diminished 5th	3	C - G$\flat$
perfect 5th	3½	C - G
augmented 5th	4	C - G$\sharp$
minor 6th	4	C - A$\flat$
major 6th	4½	C - A
minor 7th	5	C - B$\flat$
major 7th	5½	C - B
octave	6	C - C$^{/}$ **

*only possible on stringed instruments, where the same note can be played in two different places.

** the interval between one note and the same note an octave higher.

Certain intervals are more commonly used than others. In rock music, the perfect fifth is frequently used in rhythm guitar playing (power chords). Heavy rock riffs often use perfect fifths and fourths singly or in combination. Jazz guitarists like using octaves to thicken single-note melody lines whereas thirds and sixths are the intervals most commonly used in vocal harmonies.

Here are some intervals, with the bottom note as C:

7. MODES

So far we have looked at the major scale, and the natural, harmonic and melodic minor scales. The major scale and the natural minor were both known to the ancient Greeks. They called the major scale the Ionian mode and the natural minor the Aeolian mode. There were five other modes, which are occasionally used in popular music today.

The Dorian Mode

The Dorian mode is the pattern of intervals found in the sequence D - D on the white notes of the keyboard.

Dorian mode

D   E   F   G   A   B   C   D

If this is compared with D natural minor –

D natural minor

D   E   F   G   A   B♭   C   D

– you can see that one note is different, B instead of B♭. So the Dorian mode can be thought of as the natural minor with a sharpened 6th.

The dorian scale sounds edgier than the natural minor and is favoured by bands like Santana.

The Phrygian Mode

The Phrygian mode is the pattern of intervals found in the sequence E - E on the white notes of the keyboard.

If this is compared with E natural minor –

– you can see that one note is different, F instead of F♯. So the Phrygian mode can be thought of as the natural minor with a flattened second.

The Lydian Mode

The Lydian mode is the pattern of intervals found in the sequence F - F on the white notes of the keyboard.

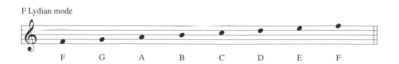

If this is compared with F major –

F Major

F   G   A   B♭   C   D   E   F

– you can see that one note is different, B instead of B♭. So the Lydian mode can be thought of as the major with a sharpened 4th.

The Mixolydian Mode

The Mixolydian mode is the pattern of intervals found in the sequence G - G on the white notes of the piano.

G Mixolydian mode

G   A   B   C   D   E   F   G

If this is compared with G major –

G Major

G   A   B   C   D   E   F♯   G

– you can see that one note is different, F instead of F♯. So the Mixolydian mode can be thought of as the major scale with a flattened 7th.

Since much pop and rock is blues-influenced, and since blues often flattens the seventh of the scale, the mixolydian is the most common of these five modes.

The Locrian Mode

The Locrian mode is the pattern of intervals found in the sequence B - B on the white notes of the piano.

If this is compared with B natural minor –

– you can see that two notes have been changed, C instead of C♯, and F instead of F♯. So the Locrian mode can be thought of as the natural minor with a flattened 2nd and 5th. This means that the Locrian scale is the furthest from the normal major or minor scale and is therefore quite uncommon.

Transposing Modes

Any mode can be transposed onto any note. It is possible to have a C dorian, C phrygian, C lydian, C mixolydian or C locrian scale. Accidentals may need to be used to make the gaps between the notes match those between the notes of the mode as indicated before.

Here's an example of the Dorian scale, in C:

C Dorian mode

| C | D | E♭ | F | G | A | B♭ | C |

Some Other Scales

There are many other types of scale used in different cultures around the world. Here's a quick look at some scales used commonly in rock, pop and blues.

Pentatonic Scale

There are two main types of pentatonic scale. The pentatonic major is merely an edited form of the major scale using 1, 2, 3, 5 and 6.

Here's an example in G:

G major pentatonic

| G | A | B | D | E | G |

Minor Pentatonic Scale

The pentatonic minor is an edited form of the natural minor scale using 1, 3, 4, 5, and 7.

G minor pentatonic

G   B♭   C   D   F   G

Minor 6th Pentatonic Scale

Here's another interesting sound – take away the 7th and add the natural 6th to the minor pentatonic to create the minor 6th pentatonic.

G minor 6 pentatonic

G   B♭   C   D   E   G

Blues Scale

Finally, here's what's known as the 'Blues' scale: a sort of pentatonic minor scale with an added sharpened fourth. Check out the sound of this – some blues players never use anything else!

G Blues scale

G   B♭   C   C♯   D   F   G

8.   CHORDS

Most music consists of melody, rhythm and harmony – and harmony depends on chords. The next thing we need to look at is how a chord is formed.

What is a chord?

A simple chord involves three different notes and is also known as a triad. In making a triad the distance between the 1st and middle note, and between the middle and top note, must be an interval of a major or minor third (major third = 2 tones, minor third = 1½ tones.)

Here are the four triad types:

Major triad	C		E		G
intervals		2		1½	

Minor triad	C		E♭		G
intervals		1½		2	

Augmented triad	C		E		G♯
intervals		2		2	

Diminished triad	C		E♭		G♭
intervals		1½		1½	

C major   C minor   C augmented   C diminished

The interval gaps are reversed between major and minor. Notice that while the root note and fifth remain the same, the only difference between a major chord and a minor is the note in the middle, the 'third' of the chord. These triads can be formed on any of the 12 notes.

These four triad types have different qualities, and this is one of the reasons music is able to evoke complex feelings. For example, the minor triad seems sad in comparison to the major. Most songs use a combination of major and minor chords.

The augmented and diminished chords are used occasionally, in certain specific contexts. A diminished chord has interval gaps of two minor thirds which makes it closer to the minor than the major - whereas the augmented triad has interval gaps of two major thirds, which makes it closer to the major.

Voicings

If we take the notes of the C major and C minor triads and write them on the stave you can see that many different combinations of the three notes are possible. These variations are called voicings, and modify the effect of the chord.

Inversions

The sound of a chord is also affected by which note is lowest. All of the above examples used C (or the root note) as the lowest note. This is what is known as a *root position* chord.

Consider the next examples.

1st   1st   2nd   2nd

If the third of the chord (E for C major, E♭ for C minor) is placed at the bottom of the chord, we create a *first inversion* – meaning simply to 'turn upside down'. If the fifth of the chord is placed at the bottom, we have created a *second inversion*.

With a simple triad, only the root position and first and second inversions are possible. If the chord had four notes in it then it would be possible to have a third inversion – and so on. The number of possible inversions is always one less than the number of notes in the chord.

Relating Chords To Keys - Major

The chords that belong to a major or minor key are derived from its scale. Let's investigate. Here's the scale of C major with the notes of the scale numbered:

By taking the 1st, 3rd and 5th notes of the scale, we get a triad of C major, C E G. If we then do the same thing with D, using the same notes of the scale, we get D F A, the chord of D minor. By doing the same thing on every note of the scale we form the seven chords of the key:

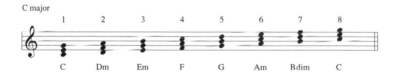

Here are the chords of A major.

And here are the primary chords in E♭ major.

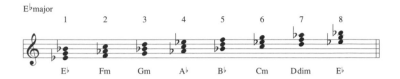

We can use a sort of shorthand to talk about each of these seven chords regardless of which key we happen to be in. We can call the chords by the degrees of the scale in roman numerals - chords I, II, III, IV, V, VI and VII. As all major scales have the same internal musical relationships the sequence of chords always follows the pattern:

major   minor   minor   major   major   minor   diminished

Minor Key Chords

The formation of the chords in a minor key depends on which minor scale we use. Let's take the natural minor scale first.

The Natural Minor

In each case the primary seven chords follow this pattern:

minor   diminished   major   minor   minor   major   major

Here are the primary chords in A natural minor.

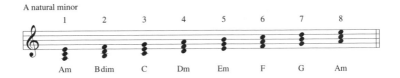

Here are the primary chords in F♯ natural minor.

Here are the primary chords in C natural minor.

The Harmonic Minor

If, however, we use the harmonic minor form we get a slightly different result. In each case the seven chords follow this pattern:

minor   diminished   augmented   minor   major   major   diminished

This different pattern has been caused by the sharpened seventh note, in the harmonic minor scale. Here are some examples:

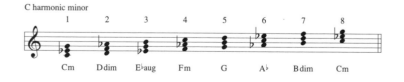

Beyond Triads

So far we have just looked at simple major and minor triads. More complex chords can be built by simply adding more notes to the triad, or altering the top note (the fifth).

Sevenths

Here's one way of extending the basic triad. By adding the seventh note in the scale, we create a 7th chord.

If we did this with the first six chords in the major scale we would end up with a sequence like this:

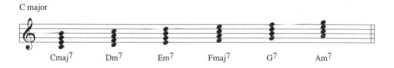

There are three types of chord here: let's look at these.

Dominant Seventh   C E G B♭   1 3 5 ♭7

The most common type of these three chords is the dominant seventh. To form the dominant seventh simply flatten the seventh note of the scale and add it to the triad. It naturally occurs only on the fifth (dominant) note of the major scale and has a tougher sound than the major seventh.

In blues and blues-influenced music where flattened notes are introduced into the harmony, the dominant seventh chord is frequently built on chords I, IV or V.

Major Seventh   C E G B   1 3 5 7

The major seventh naturally occurs in the first and fourth notes of the major scale. It has a rich, expressive sound.

Minor Seventh   C E♭ G B♭   1 ♭3 5 ♭7

The minor seventh naturally occurs on the second, third and sixth notes of the major scale. It has a melancholy sound but is softer than a straight minor chord.

Suspended Chords

Here's another way of altering the sound of basic triads. Suspended chords (sus2 and sus4) are formed by taking away the third degree of the scale – so the chord is neither major or minor– and adding the fourth or second, to create a 'suspension' in the harmony. They are commonly 'resolved' to either a major or minor chord, depending on the key of the piece.

First Octave Chords

Here are the most common types of chord formed by just using a single octave major scale:

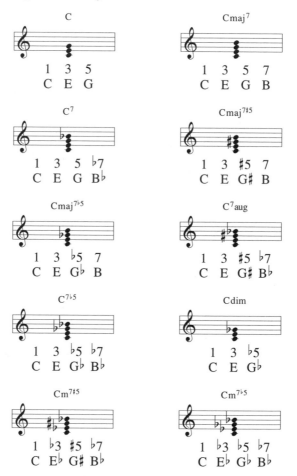

First Octave Chords (cont.)

Cm♭6

1	♭3	5	♭6
C	E♭	G	A♭

Cm6

1	♭3	5	6
C	E♭	G	A

Caug

1	3	♯5
C	E	G♯

Cdim7

1	♭3	♭5	♭♭7
C	E♭	G♭	B♭♭

C6

1	3	5	6
C	E	G	A

Csus2

1	2	5
C	D	G

Csus4

1	4	5
C	F	G

Cm

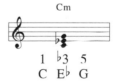

1	♭3	5
C	E♭	G

Cm7

1	♭3	5	♭7
C	E♭	G	B♭

Cm(maj7)

1	♭3	5	7
C	E♭	G	B

To form more complex chords we can extend the scale to a second octave:

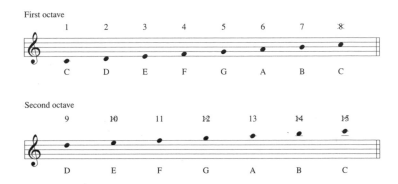

Of these notes only the 9th, 11 and 13th are meaningful - the 8th, 10th, 12th and 15th notes are simply notes of the basic major triad, an octave higher. They don't 'stand out' or alter the sound of the chord in the same way as a 9th or 11th. The 14th is also irrelevant, as the 7th is used instead.

Second Octave Chords

Here are some examples of second octave chords. Many of these are rarely encountered with every note present. In popular music and jazz, a 13th chord rarely has the 11th also present (as it produces a clash with the 3rd). Similarly, 11th chords usually omit the 3rd.

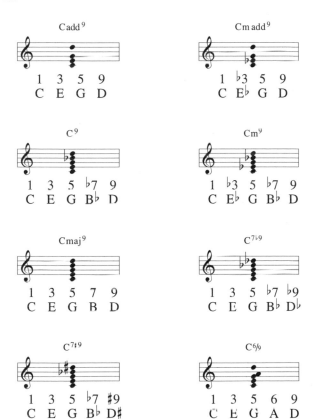

Cadd⁹

1	3	5	9
C	E	G	D

Cm add⁹

1	♭3	5	9
C	E♭	G	D

C⁹

1	3	5	♭7	9
C	E	G	B♭	D

Cm⁹

1	♭3	5	♭7	9
C	E♭	G	B♭	D

Cmaj⁹

1	3	5	7	9
C	E	G	B	D

C⁷♭⁹

1	3	5	♭7	♭9
C	E	G	B♭	D♭

C⁷♯⁹

1	3	5	♭7	♯9
C	E	G	B♭	D♯

C⁶⁄₉

1	3	5	6	9
C	E	G	A	D

Second Octave Chords (cont.)

Cm¹¹

1	♭3	5	♭7	9	11
C	E♭	G	B♭	D	F

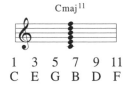

Cmaj¹¹

1	3	5	7	9	11
C	E	G	B	D	F

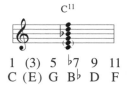

C¹¹

1	(3)	5	♭7	9	11
C	(E)	G	B♭	D	F

C⁷add¹¹

1	3	5	♭7	11
C	E	G	B♭	F

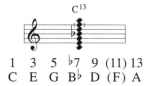

C¹³

1	3	5	♭7	9	(11)	13
C	E	G	B♭	D	(F)	A

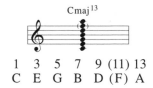

Cmaj¹³

1	3	5	7	9	(11)	13
C	E	G	B	D	(F)	A

Cm¹³

1	♭3	5	♭7	9	11	13
C	E♭	G	B♭	D	F	A

Part 2.
Musical Terms

A capella

(I) Lit. 'in a church manner'. Music sung by unaccompanied voices.

A tempo

(I) Return to the original speed.

Accelerando

(I) Gradually increase the tempo.

Accent

A small arrow-like mark placed on a note or **chord** giving it more emphasis.

Acciaccatura

(I) Lit. 'crushed'. A note that theoretically has no duration, added before another as a decoration.

Accidental

A **sharp** (♯), **flat** (♭) or **natural** (♮) sign which raises or lowers a note by a **semitone**, or restores it to its usual pitch respectively.

Acoustic

(i) The sound characteristics of a room.
(ii) Any instrument designed for use without an amplifier.

Action

The height of the strings from the fretboard or neck of a stringed instrument, especially the guitar.

Ad lib.

(L) Improvise a section or repeat a phrase with extempore variations.

Adagio

(I) Lit. 'at ease'. Slow tempo - faster than Largo, slower than Andante.

ADT

Automatic Double Tracking. Recording technique used to thicken a vocal line or instrument. The part is re-recorded onto an adjacent track, with a slightly different echo or other effect, to create the illusion of two voices or instruments.

Aeolian

One of seven Greek scales, the Aeolian **mode** is the **interval** sequence A B C D E F G A. Also known as the 'natural minor' **scale**.

Air

A term that occurs initially in French and English music in the C16th to describe a **melody** or song. It is found in the music of Dowland, Campion and Purcell.

Allegro

(I) Lit. 'cheerful'. Lively, quick tempo. Allegretto is slightly slower than allegro.

Allemande

A popular Baroque dance, also known as an 'alman', which in the C16th formed part of the **Suite**'s structure.

Altered chord

A **chord** in which a note or notes are changed chromatically. Thus, the **chord** C7($\flat$5) (C E G$\flat$ B$\flat$) has had the fifth (G) flattened by a **semitone**.

Alto

(I) Lit. 'high'. High male or low female voice part spanning from G at the top of the bass clef to the C above **middle** C.

Ambient

Term popular in the 1990s to describe electronic music which has a dreamy atmosphere assisted by extensive use of **reverb** in the mix. Main proponents include The Orb and Brian Eno.

Anacrusis

Term to describe an unstressed note or notes at the start of a piece of music or phrase.

Andante

(I) Lit. 'going'. At a moderate **tempo**, or walking pace. Between allegretto and **adagio.**

Animato

(I) Played in a lively, spirited manner.

Anticipation

Playing a note slightly early, or generally describing an effect of **syncopation**.

Antiphony

An arrangement in which a piece of music uses two groups of performers to generate a 'call-and-response' structure.

Anthem

Choral composition deriving from the Latin motet, written for performance in church. Usually, but not necessarily, accompanied by organ.

A. O. R.

Adult Oriented Rock. Mildly derogatory term for a type of commercial rock music chiefly popular in the U.S. during the 1970s and 1980s and played by groups such as Fleetwood Mac, Boston, Foreigner, etc. See also **M. O. R.**

Appoggiatura

(I) 'leaning note'. A type of grace-note which creates a brief dissonance before resolving down to the next note. The appoggiatura is usually a tone or **semitone** above the main note.

Augmented

The augmented **triad** (C E G♯) is comprised of two major thirds. Also used of a note which has been sharpened within a **chord**: C7 (C E G B♭) becomes C7aug (C E G♯ B♭).

Aria

(I) 'style or manner'. A song or song-like piece associated with opera, usually in three sections, A.B.A. If the middle section is omitted, an arietta.

Arpeggio

Figure in which the notes of a **chord** are played one after the other rather than simultaneously.

Atonality

Music written without the organising principle of **keys**, **scales** and **harmony**.

B

Backing track

Piece of music used for singing over, and as such an instrumental mix of a song. This is also the meaning when the term is used in a recording studio. These have been popularised through karaoke machines. Backing tracks are also frequently used for performers to mime with on TV appearances.

Backline

The amplifiers arranged at the back of the stage for individual musicians. Contrasts with the monitor / **foldback** system and the P.A.

Backward guitar

Recording technique popularised in the 1960s. Reels of tape are taken off a reel-to-reel tape recorder and reversed. The guitarist then solos in the appropriate section, starting where the solo is meant to end and ending where the solo will start. When the tape is put back the right way, the notes are reversed, coming in quietly then suddenly cutting off.

Ballad/Ballade

A song telling a story in which each verse is set to the same music. The Ballade is a romantic piece for a single instrument, a title used by composers like Brahms and Schumann.

Bar

Line placed across the **stave** that divides music into rhythmic sections. The first beat of each **bar** always carries slightly more emphasis.

Barre

(F) Fretting technique on the guitar where a finger (usually the first) is laid flat on the neck to hold down more than one string.

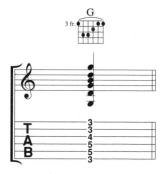

Baritone
Lit. 'Deep-sounding'. A **bass** voice of medium-low pitch, spanning from the F♯ above **middle C** down nearly two octaves to A.

Baroque
European music of the period 1600-1750, notable composers include J.S. Bach, Vivaldi, Purcell, Corelli, Handel and Scarlatti.

Bass
(i) Lowest part of a musical composition, significant for stabilising and defining the **harmony**.
(ii) Male voice part spanning F below the bass clef to D above **middle C**.

Bass drum
Along with the snare, the most important part of the drum kit, supplying a low frequency 'thud' which is offset by the higher frequency 'crack' of the snare. Most drum patterns in popular music are characterised by a variety of subtle patterns of the two.

Bass guitar
Devised in the 1950s as a convenient alternative to the double bass, the bass guitar has the same notes as the lower four strings of the guitar (EADG), but an octave lower. The electric bass is a vital part of the rhythm section in popular music. Acoustic bass guitars are also sometimes used.

Beatbox
(Colloq.) Electronic drum machine used in modern dance music.

Bend
A smooth change in pitch, usually up by a half or whole step, used on guitar, harmonica, and synthesiser.

Bi-amping
Form of amplification using sophisticated equipment that allows specific frequencies to be sent to more than one speaker according to which speaker is designed for which frequency. This is contrast to traditional amp/speaker configurations where a single type of speaker has to convey the whole signal.

Binary form
The balanced halves of a dance movement.

Bitonality
The use of two different **keys** at the same time.

Black note

The five black keys of the piano - C♯ D♯ F♯ G♯ A♯ and their respective flats, D♭ E♭ G♭ A♭ and B♭.

Blue note

Harmonic effect crucial to **blues** or blues-derived music. The singer or soloist deliberately pitches a note a **semitone flat** for the **key**, creating the moody tension typical of the **blues**. The commonest blue notes are the flattened 3rd and flattened 7th - in C major (C D E F G A B) E♭ and B♭.

Blues

Popular Afro-American vocal and instrumental music with emotional roots in the black experience of social oppression. It began as a rural music in the Mississippi delta, the first recordings dating back to the 1920s. The migration of many blacks to northern cities led to the development of an urban, electric blues typified by Muddy Waters and Howlin' Wolf. The constituent parts of blues music are extremely simple yet capable of bearing the imprint of a host of individual voices. The main forms are 8, 12, 16 or 32 bars, using **chords** I, IV and V, often as **dominant** 7s. The melodic content exhibits the use of the flattened 3rd, 5th and 7th of the **scale**, these notes deliberately clashing with the major tonality underneath. Blues enjoyed a significant revival in the 1960s when British rock musicians such as Eric Clapton and John Mayall introduced it to a wider audience by recording blues songs and appearing with the likes of John Lee Hooker, Howlin' Wolf and B. B. King.

Bolero

Type of Spanish dance in triple time now forever associated with the languid modal **melody** and the strident, obsessive rhythms of Ravel's composition and in rock music with 'Beck's Bolero' (1968) by guitarists Jeff Beck and Jimmy Page.

Boogie-woogie

Type of rhythmic **blues** popular in the mid-C20th, chiefly for piano. The right hand is free to improvise phrases while the left hand maintains steady, repeating **bass** figures often built on **dominant** 7th **arpeggios**.

Bootleg

Unofficial recording (usually of a concert), circulated in cassette, vinyl or CD format. Despite their illegality, the legendary status of bootlegs has done much to stimulate interest in major performers and to sustain their presence in popular music long after the act in question has split up. Possibly the most famous bootleg of all time was a recording of Bob Dylan's 1966 concert at the Manchester Free Trade Hall, entitled (confusingly) *Live At The Royal Albert Hall*. Should not be confused with piracy which is the counterfeiting of officially released product.

Bottleneck

Metal or glass tube placed on the third or fourth finger of the fretting hand, used by guitarists to produce distinctive **glissando** and **vibrato** effects. Altered tunings often assist the **slide** technique, which is heard in **blues**, rock and folk music.

Bouncing

Also known as 'ping-ponging'. Technique by which a recording on, say, track 1 is re-recorded ('bounced') onto another track, sometimes as another part is added. Bounces can be single (track 1 to track 2) or multiple (tracks 1-7 onto 8), and anything in between.

Bourrée

(F) Type of French dance similar to the **Gavotte** but taken at a quicker **tempo**, in 2/2 time and starting on the last crotchet of the **bar**.

B. P. M.

Beats Per Minute. Standardised tempo indication. Indicated by a crotchet, e.g. [♩] = 120 b.p.m.

Bridge

(i) Transitional section of a song connecting verse and **chorus**, sometimes having a similar function to a middle 8. (ii) In instruments like the guitar and violin the piece of wood or metal over which the strings pass to the neck.

Broken chord

Accompaniment half way between **arpeggios** and **chord** playing. The **chords** are split up - often the root note is played first followed by the 3rd and 5th together - and unlike an **arpeggio** remain within one **octave**.

Bossa Nova

Lit. 'New Trend'; a popular Brazilian dance. Rhythm usually characterised by syncopation.

C

Cadence

(L) Lit. 'To fall' . A **chord** change which marks the end of a phrase in traditional **harmony**. There are four main types of cadence - **perfect**, **imperfect**, **plagal**, and **interrupted**.

Cadenza

Passage that occurs toward the conclusion of a **concerto** movement designed to exhibit the technical brilliance of the solo featured performer.

Calypso

Dance form with its origins in West Indian folk music, associated with Trinidad and the Caribbean.

Canon

Music in which several voices sing the same melodic line but begin and end at different times. Unlike a **round**, the second voice can enter before the first has finished its phrase, and may be transposed down or up a 4th or 5th.

Cantabile

(I) In a singing style.

Cantata

A piece of music composed for solo voices, **chorus** and **orchestra**. During the **Baroque** era it was a piece of sacred music but eventually also developed secular themes.

Capo D'astro

Abbrev. Capo. Device that wraps around a guitar neck, raising the pitch of the strings. Allows playing in difficult **keys** or in keys that suit a singer's voice, and changes the tone of the guitar making unique **chord** voicings possible high up the neck.

Catch

Tune with four phrases which can be sung simultaneously without discord. The catch is started one phrase at a time until all four are going. Examples include 'London's Burning' or 'Frère Jacques'.

Chamber music

Music written not for the concert hall but for more intimate surroundings. A typical chamber ensemble is the **string quartet**.

Chorale

Hymn-tune, most famously associated with J. S. Bach. Generations of students have learned **harmony** by fitting **chords** to Bach chorale melodies.

Chord

Group of more than two notes played together, in contrast to an **interval** which consists of only two notes. Chords produce **harmony**, in contrast to the rhythmic and melodic components of music.

Chorus

(i) In **classical** music, singers supply vocal sections in a longer work.
(ii) In popular music, the most memorable section of a song, often repeated.
(iii) Electronic **delay** effect that slightly alters pitch of original signal, creating a distinctive thickening of the sound.

Chromatic

A note or **chord** which does not normally occur within the **key**. Thus in C major the notes C♯, D♯, F♯, G♯ and A♯ are all chromatic. Chromaticism is the extensive use of such notes or chords to extend the **harmony**.

Circle of fifths

Progression of the **keys** in a circle. Starting at C major, the major **keys** progress by fifths (3 1/2 tones) to G, D, A, E, B, F♯, C♯. B is also C♭, F♯ is G♭, C# is Db, and continuing in fifths gives A♭, E♭, B, F and finally C, thus completing the circle.

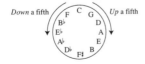

Classical

Term used popularly and imprecisely of any music classified as 'high culture' or 'serious', played on traditional orchestral instruments from written parts. More correctly, European music of the mid-eighteenth century to the early C19th, typified by Mozart, Haydn and early Beethoven.

Music from the Classical period has a well-defined **harmony** and strong interest in maintaining and establishing formal rules of composition.

Clef

(F) key. A sign placed on the **stave** to fix the pitch of the lines. The G treble clef fixes the second line as G, the F bass clef fixes the fourth line as F. There are also C alto clefs and tenor clefs.

Treble clef	Alto clef	Bass clef

Click bass

Popular electric bass style of the late 1960s / early 1970s defined both by tone - a trebly sound and the use of a pick - and stylistically by an imitation of the eighth-note **syncopation** of the **Motown** bassist James Jamerson.

Coda

Lit. 'tail'. The final section of a piece of music culminating in the last **bar**.

Compact Disc
(CD). Digital recording format on which information stored on a disk is read by a laser.

Common time
Another term for 4/4 time, four crotchet beats in a bar.

Comping
(Colloq.) Providing a simple chordal accompaniment to a soloist. Also known as vamping.

Compound interval
Distance between two notes greater than an **octave**. A major **ninth** is the compound version of a major 2nd.

Major 2nd   Major 9th

Compound Time
A time-signature in which the basic pulse or beat is divisible by three. E.g: 6/8, 9/8, 12/8. See also **simple time** and **duple time**.

Compression
Sound effect used in recordings to increase the volume of quieter sounds and limit louder ones so as to prevent peak signals which would otherwise spoil a recording.

Concert pitch
Universal reference in which the note A is taken as having a **frequency** of 440Hz.

Concerto
Large-scale concert work in three movements usually featuring **orchestra** and a solo instrument.

Consonance
Combinations of notes pleasing to the ear. The **intervals** of major and minor 3rd and 6th are consonant. Opposite of **dissonance**.

Contrary motion
Effect caused by two melodic lines moving in opposite directions. Contrasts with oblique motion where one voice remains on the same note while the other moves.

Contrapuntal
Music in which several melodic lines move independently of each other yet still sustain a sense of harmonic organisation in terms of the **chords** they produce or imply. Counterpoint is a more rigidly defined type of contrapuntal music, having specific rules governing the movement of the different parts.

Counter-tenor

Lit. 'Against the tenor'. The highest male voice, not to be confused with male alto or falsetto.

Crescendo

Direction for music to increase in volume.

Crosstalk

Unwanted sound heard on analogue **multi-track** recordings where, owing to the existence of parallel tracks on tape, some of the signal on one track can be heard on an adjacent track at high volume or during very quiet passages.

Crotchet

Quarter-note, four of which make a **bar** of 4/4 time.

Cutaway

Contouring of the guitar-body to make notes on the high frets more accessible easily. The Gibson Les Paul is a single cutaway guitar, the Fender Stratocaster a double cutaway.

Examples of cutaway:

Fender Stratocaster - double cutaway

Gibson Les Paul - single cutaway

D

Da capo al fine
(I) Return to the beginning and play through until the end.

Dal segno al fine
(I) Return to the dal segno sign (*D.S.*) and play through to the end.

D.A.T.
Digital Audio Tape. Trademarked name for a type of audio tape on which digital information can be stored on two tracks.

Decibel
Abbrev. dB. A unit for measuring relative levels of power, voltage and sound intensity, and hence an objective indication of loudness.

Delay
Effect originally called 'echo', in which a note or sound is recorded and then played back at differing volumes to the original note.

Demo
Composer's initial recording, not intended for release, sometimes recorded quickly and with limited arrangement, for personal reference or to attract the interest of music publishers or record companies.

Development
Technique in **classical** music whereby a musical idea is extended and changed, essential to longer works such as concertos and symphonies.

Diatonic
Intervals or **chords** derived from notes in or related to the tonic scale, in contrast to **chromatic**.

Diminished
Opposite to **augmented**. Refers to any **triad**, e.g. C E♭ G♭ in which the **intervals** are two minor 3rds. If a further note is added B♭♭ (A) another minor 3rd up, the diminished 7th **chord** is formed. The diminished **triad** naturally occurs as **chord** VII in a major **key** (in C major, B D F).

Diminuendo
Direction for music to get quieter in volume.

Dirge
General term for any slow piece of a mournful nature, especially connected with death and funerals.

Disco

Style of singles-oriented dance music popular in the mid-70s, celebrated in the film Saturday Night Fever. Disco is typified by a four-to-the-**bar** bass drum beat and pronounced eighth-note, or quaver, octaves in the bass.

Disjunct motion

Motion in leaps rather than in steps.

Dissonance

Opposite of **consonance**. A dissonance is a sound which is traditionally perceived as not harmonious. The minor **second** C-C♯, augmented 4th C-F♯ and major 7th C-B are dissonant **intervals**.

C-B

Dominant

The fifth note and **chord** of the **major scale**.

Dominant (G)
Chord of G

Dorian

One of the seven Greek **modes** or scales, the Dorian **mode** is the **interval** sequence D E F G A B C D (a natural minor scale with a raised 6th).

D   E   F   G   A   B   C   D

Dot

A dot placed after a note increases the duration of that note by 50%. A dotted **crotchet** [♩.] is therefore a **crotchet** plus a **quaver**. Similarly, a double dot increases the duration of the note by half plus a quarter, therefore a double-dotted **minim** equals a **minim**, plus a **crotchet**, plus a **quaver**.

Downbeat

The first beat of the **bar**, and also the third beat in 4/4. It contrasts with the upbeat (beats 2 and 4) and the off-beat which in 4/4 is represented by even numbered eighth notes.

Drone

Note or group of notes played repeatedly to support a **melody** or changing **chords**. Drones are often found in non-Western music, especially those which have an emphasis on **melody** but not on **harmony**.

Drop-in

Recording technique for correcting mistakes. The musician plays along with the recorded part and the engineer starts recording at the moment where the mistake occurred. Once the musician has supplied the correct notes, the engineer cancels the record mode.

Dry
An original sound signal without any effects processing (such as **reverb**). Contrasts with **wet**.

Duple time
2/4 time or two beats in a **bar**. See also **compound** and **simple** time.

Dynamics
The understanding and use of volume in music, contrasting loud and quiet passages. e.g:
p = soft (piano)
f = loud (forte)
mf = moderately loud (mezzoforte)

E

Early Music

Term that describes both a period and an attitude towards the interpretation and performance of music. Generally means music up to about 1650, especially those composers and works neglected because their music was written for obsolete instruments such as the lute and viol. It became popular to play this music with the greatest possible authenticity, using faithful reproductions of antique instruments and attempting to expunge from performance any assumptions about expression which were the product of later centuries.

E-bow

Battery-powered device held in a guitarist's picking hand which causes the string to produce an endlessly sustained note.

Effects unit

Electrical circuit, analogue or digital, designed to modify sound. They range from small, single-effect units turned on and off with footswitches, to complex multi-parameter programmable modules. Used with most electric instruments, though when used as part of the recording / mixing process, they can alter the sound of instruments with an acoustic source.

Electric guitar

Version of the classical (Spanish) and steel-strung acoustic instrument which relies on magnetic pickups for much of its sound. The vibrating strings create fluctuations in the magnetic field which in turn are converted into an electric signal strengthened by an amplifier and so rendered audible by a speaker. The electric guitar can be solid or semi-solid. It is tuned in the same manner as the acoustic guitar, although it tends to be strung with lighter gauge strings. Very few instruments have the potential to move as much air and generate as much sound as the electric guitar. Originally conceived simply as a loud guitar, the electric guitar has developed a sound all its own and is the central instrument of rock music.

Electro-acoustic

Type of acoustic guitar developed in the 1970s-80s to get round the problem of amplifying through a microphone in a concert. The electro-acoustic has a built-in pickup and usually some form of volume and tone controls to enable the sound of the guitar to pass direct into an amplifier or P.A. Recently, nylon-strung examples have appeared.

Enharmonic

In certain musical situations such as a key-change, a note can change its name without changing its pitch. In a key-change from E minor to E♭ major, the D♯ of E minor becomes E♭ of the new **key**. This is an enharmonic change,

Enhancer

Sound processing unit found in studios designed to add extra overall 'sparkle' to a **mix**, or to give one instrument greater prominence.

Equal temperament

A tuning system based on dividing the **octave** into twelve equal parts. See **temperament**.

Equalisation

Abbrev. E.Q. Mixing process either during recording or at a live concert where different frequencies can be cut or boosted, to set the tonal balance.

Étude

(Fr. 'Study'). A piece of variable form designed to allow the performer or student to exercise an aspect of technique.

Exposition

Initial statement of a musical theme which is then subject to **development**.

Fader
Sliding control on a mixing desk or similar by which a signal's level is increased or reduced.

Falsetto
Type of singing used by male vocalists to extend the upward range of their voices. The falsetto voice uses only part of the vocal chords and is therefore weaker than the normal voice. It can produce delicate, expressive and shrill effects.

Fanfare
Short piece of music usually played on brass instruments at a ceremonial occasion. More generally understood to be the introduction to, or homage to, a person or event.

Feedback
Noise created when an amplified note is fed back into the electrical system which produced it in the first place. This causes the note to sustain, increase in volume and often 'decay' into one of its higher **harmonics**.

Figured bass
Notation system by which numbers written in the **bass** indicate the type of **chord** intended to harmonise that bass note.

Finale
Last movement of a longer piece of music with several movements.

Fine
(I) Lit. 'the end'.

Fingering
Process of interpretation in which an instrumentalist chooses which fingers to use to play each note in a piece in order to produce the best performance.

Flam
Technique used by drummers in which the snare drum is struck by both sticks a fraction of a second apart, creating a dramatic effect.

Flamenco
Popular folk-music of Spain, featuring dancing and a **virtuoso** guitar technique combining vigorous strumming, percussive tapping of the guitar body, and **Phrygian** melodies.

Flanging
Sound effect used on electric guitar involving a moving sweep of frequencies (similar to phasing).

Flat
Accidental placed in front of a note, lowering it by a **semitone**.

B   B flat

Foldback

Arrangement of speakers at the front and side of a stage which projects sound back to the performers, enabling them to hear themselves.

Folk Baroque

Term coined to describe the ornate fingerstyle of 1960s folk guitarists such as John Renbourn, Bert Jansch and Davey Graham.

Folk music

Term which covers an enormous variety of music but which is generally understood to be 'of the people' and tends therefore to be defined against 'high' or 'serious' music. Folk music in its traditional form is a body of music - songs, melodies, dances and lyrics - which expresses the sensibility and experiences of the mass of a population using acoustic, low-tech instruments and a relatively simple musical aesthetic of form and harmony. Interest in folk melodies has been shown from time to time by 'serious' composers. There was a revival of folk music after World War II. Some would argue that commercial pop, rock and soul has superseded the folk music of the twentieth century.

Folk rock

Hybrid of Anglo-American folk music developed in the 1960s. It involves the arrangement of traditional material for variations on the rock line-up of acoustic and electric guitar, bass and drums, with electric violin and mandolin sometimes present. The chief exponents include Fairport Convention and Steeleye Span in the UK, Alan Stivell in France, and The Byrds in the US. The term is more loosely applied to rock music with a softer, more acoustic approach.

Forte

(I) Play loudly.

Fortepiano

(i) Successor to the harpsichord and forerunner of the modern 'grand' piano. (ii) As a playing direction, means to play loudly then quietly.

Frequency

The rate of vibration of a sounding body or instrument, measured in cycles per second (Hertz). Frequency increases with pitch, doubling every octave.

Fret

A thin piece of metal, wood or ivory laid across and hammered into a fingerboard which marks the place where the finger is placed to produce a note of that pitch. Frets are found on instruments such as the guitar, mandolin and banjo. 'To fret' means to hold down a note on such a fingerboard.

Fretless bass

Type of electric bass guitar with the frets removed, facilitating pitch-smooth glissandos and similar expressive effects. The sound was popularised by Jaco Pastorius in the 1970s.

Fugue

Complex **baroque** work usually for keyboard involving the statement and **development** of musical themes which overlap in a precise manner. The most famous examples are Bach's Forty-Eight Preludes and Fugues.

Fundamental note

The most important **frequency** in a note, in contrast to the **overtones** which are also present but not as audible.

Funk

Originally used in the 1950s among jazz musicians, the term is now associated with a sub-genre of commercial black music developed out of R'n'B by James Brown in the 1960s and popularised in the 1970s. This is an earthy, street-wise form of soul, with strong bass and rhythms, especially an emphasis on the first down beat of the bar, and 'looped' motifs.

FX

Abbrev. for audio effects.

G

Gain
Control on a studio mixing desk which increases the input level on that channel. On guitar amplifiers this increases the distortion.

Galliard
A popular sixteenth century dance, usually lively and in 3/4 time. The name was also used for pieces played on instruments such as the Elizabethan Galliard.

Garage band
Term to describe a primitive style of rock music, usually played by a guitar/bass/drums line-up, consisting of loud, fast, short songs with no pretensions to be 'art' but manifesting instead a 'trash' aesthetic. It derives from the U.S. and from the necessity of amateur bands with no money to practise in garages. The earliest garage bands date from the 1960s.

Gavotte
C18th French dance-form in 2/2 time exhibiting four-**bar** phrases which often start in the middle of the **bar**, and a lively **tempo**.

Gig
Colloquial expression for a concert or similar musical performance.

Giusto
(It.) Meaning precise or exact, normally met with in the phrase 'tempo giusto', telling the performer to keep the time strict.

Glam rock
Singles-oriented music popular in the UK from 1971-74, typified by David Bowie, T. Rex, and Roxy Music. Glam rejected both the musical pretentions of progressive rock and the introspection of the singer-songwriters. It revived some musical traits of 1950s rock'n'roll and dressed them up in space-age androgyny.

Glissando
An ascending or descending **slur** of notes progressing in a continuous raising or lowering of pitch.

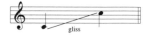

Glued-neck
Element of electric guitar construction where the neck is glued into place, in contrast to the 'bolt-on' design. The Gibson Les Paul has a glued-neck, the Fender Stratocaster a bolt-on neck.

Grace-notes

Notes added to the main note to add musical interest, including the **acciaccatura**, **appoggiatura**, mordent and trill.

Acciaccatura   Mordent

Turn   Trill

Gospel

Influential style of Afro-American vocal music originally sung by black congregations during church services, unaccompanied or with clapping or minimal instrumental accompaniment from piano or organ. The vocal style is blues-influenced, impassioned and communitarian in ethic, allowing individual voices to decorate short phrases at will. Call-and-response techniques also feature. Gospel was a vital part of 1960s soul music as can be heard in the recordings of artists such as Aretha Franklin and the Edwin Hawkins singers.

Graphic Equaliser

Or 'Graphic E.Q.': a sound processing unit that enables very fine adjustments to be made to different frequencies. These are divided into a number of 'bands'.

Gregorian chant

Early form of Western sacred vocal music named after Pope Gregory (590-604AD) utilising unaccompanied unison singing in an accentless free time.

Groove

Slang expression in popular music to describe the subtler rhythms in a song or piece of music. It refers to the human 'feel' element in a performance, in particular slight anticipations and delaying of the beat. The word is invariably approving.

Grunge

Style of rock music which enjoyed considerable success in the early 1990s, arising from the Seattle music scene and exemplified by the band Nirvana. Grunge took the **riffs** of heavy rock but replaced its guitar **virtuoso** ethos with the anarchic mentality of **punk**. Almost single-handedly this created a revolution in US rock, but Grunge never recovered from the death of Kurt Cobain, Nirvana's singer/guitarist, in April 1994.

Half-note

U.S. term for a **minim** or two-beat note in **simple time**.

1 - 2   1 - 2

Harmonics

Generally these are **overtones** which form part of a note, sounding above the **fundamental**. More specifically, 'ghost' notes that can be found at certain points along a string. See **Fundamental**.

Harmonisation

The process of taking a melodic line and adding **chords** to it.

Harmony

(i) The underlying **chord** structures of a piece of music usually based in a chosen **key** or mixture of keys.

(ii) In a vocal context the addition of backing voices to a **melody**, often a third or sixth away from the **melody** note.

Heavy Metal

Style of rock music in 1980s which evolved from late 60s hard / heavy rock, exemplified by bands such as Iron Maiden, AC/DC and Metallica. 'HM'

features repetitive slogging beats and low-pitched guitar phrases (**riffs**), frequent and extensive guitar solos and growled vocals, with morbid lyrics focusing on death and destruction.

Heavy Rock

Style of rock which developed out of the high volume rock / blues of the 1967-69 period. Songs came to be structured around repeated guitar figures played at a low pitch and often constructed from the pentatonic minor and blues scales. High volume levels and increasing stretches of guitar soloing encouraged vocalists to pitch ever higher in an effort to compete and use the voice as another instrument. Powerful drumming was another factor. Heavy rock is in some ways the less pretentious side of progressive rock. Typical bands include Led Zeppelin, Deep Purple and Black Sabbath.

Hexachord

Not actually a chord but a scale consisting of the first six notes of the major scale (in C major: C D E F G A).

Hi-hat

Part of a drum-kit, the hi-hat is a foot-operated unit consisting of two matched cymbals facing each other which can be opened and closed, and played with a stick. The hi-hat serves an important background time-keeping function, since it is often played to generate a continuous stream of eighth notes.

Hip-hop

Form of popular black music which developed out of the clubs of New York in the late 1980s in which the DJ becomes an ersatz musician 'playing' a multi-deck turntable, and manually manipulating vinyl records ('scratching'), Drum-loops, rapping, and improvisation are other elements of this dance music.

Home triad

Another expression for the key chord.

Hook

(Colloq.) Expression in popular songwriting for the melodic, lyric or harmonic idea most likely to imprint itself on a listener after hearing it only once or twice.

Humbucker

Type of **pick-up** for the electric guitar developed in the 1950s with two magnetic coils (hence 'double-coil') which 'buck the hum' endemic to single coil **pick-ups**. Humbuckers are quieter than single coils and have a thicker, less trebly tone.

Hungarian Scale

The harmonic minor scale with an augmented fourth. In C: C D E♭ F♯ G A♭ B C. The presence of two leaps of 1½ tones (3-4, 6-7) gives the scale an exotic sound.

I

true to pitch. On fretted instruments such as the guitar, intonation indicates whether adjustment to the neck is necessary to make notes in tune anywhere on the neck.

Imperfect cadence

The presence of **chords** I to V at the end of a musical phrase, creating a mood of expectancy.

I - V
G   D

Interrupted cadence

A **chord** change which suggests a **perfect cadence** (V-I) and instead creates surprise by going from V to another **chord**, often VI.

V - VI
D   Em

Impromptu

Not an improvised piece but rather one characterised by impulsiveness, a title used by such C19th composers as Schumann, Chopin, Mendelssohn and Liszt.

Intelligent

Used of sound effect units, notably harmonisers, able to imitate certain musical processes. Early harmonisers for voice or guitar developed in the 1970s would add a major 3rd above every note regardless of the requirements of the **major scale**. An intelligent harmoniser will adjust to a minor or a major 3rd, depending on which is correct.

Intonation

The determining of whether a note is

Interval

Distance between two notes. The intervals of the **major scale** are: major 2nd, major 3rd, **perfect 4th**, **perfect 5th**, major 6th, major 7th, and an **octave**.

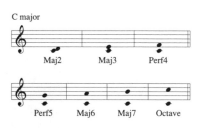

C major

Maj2   Maj3   Perf4

Perf5   Maj6   Maj7   Octave

Inversion

A simple **triad** such as C major or minor (C E G / C E♭ G) can have three forms: **root position** (where C is the

bass note), first inversion (where E or
E♭ is the **bass** note) or second inversion
(where G is the **bass** note). **Root
position chords** sound stable, first
inversions are mobile and emphasise
their tonality, whereas second inversions
are unstable.

C minor

Root   1st   2nd
inversion   inversion

Ionian
One of the seven Greek **modes** or
scales, the Ionian **mode** is the **interval**
sequence C D E F G A B C . Also
known as the **major scale**.

ips
Abbrev. for 'inches per second',
governing the speed of tape machines.

J

Jam

(Verb) Popular music slang expression for improvising. The Grateful Dead and Cream were two rock acts famous for on-stage jamming.

Jangle guitar

Style of electric guitar playing used in pop and less 'heavy' rock. The style is rhythmic and arpeggiated, exploiting the guitar's capacity for chord voicings in which notes are doubled at the same pitch. The historical origins of 'jangle guitar' lie in the playing of George Harrison of The Beatles and Roger McGuinn of The Byrds, both of whom played the Rickenbacker electric 12-string.

Jazz

Popular Afro-American music with roots in the **blues**. Initially heard as the New Orleans jazz of the 20s and 30s, it later underwent many stylistic changes establishing a range of sub-genres from 'trad jazz' to free-form, avante-garde jazz, including the big band Dixieland Revival of the 1940s, and hybrids such as jazz-funk. Jazz has a complex **harmony**, uses **swing rhythm** and **blue notes**, and places a stronger emphasis on **development** than other popular music, especially through improvisation.

Jazz-rock

Fusion of jazz and rock styles initiated from the jazz field in the mid-60s as jazz attempted to emulate some of the commercial success of rock. Notable exponents included Miles Davis, Herbie Hancock and Keith Jarrett.

Jingle

Catchy short piece of instrumental or vocal music - sometimes no more than a few seconds - used for advertising purposes.

Jug band

Small group of musicians using improvised instruments drawn from the domestic environment, such as tea-chest bass, washboard, washtub, spoons, coupled with acoustic guitar and harmonica, to play simple, infectious modern folk songs. Arising from an attempt to make the best of austere conditions, the jug band ethos clearly had an influence on skiffle.

Jumbo

Term applied to an extra large-bodied acoustic guitar. The most famous model is probably that made by Gibson, the J-200, designed in the late 1930s.

Jungle

Sub-genre of 1990s dance music, played on electronic keyboards and drum machines, featuring a stripped down and brutally rhythmic sound. Grew out of **hip-hop**, and consists primarily of speeded-up breakbeats, hence its other commonly used title, drum'n'bass.

K

Key

Sense of tonality which governs music, created by a scale and its **chords**. The C **major scale** C D E F G A B C generates the **chords** C Dm Em F G Am and B dim. A piece in C major creates a sense of key in which the key-note C and its chord subjectively feel like the centre around which everything is organised. There is aesthetic pleasure each time this 'home' chord is reached and an awareness of journeying away from it when the **harmony** moves to other **chords**. All major keys have identical internal relationships. As such, heard in isolation, they are identical, merely pitched higher or lower. However, heard in relation to each other in a key-change they create strong contrasts and a more powerful feeling of journeying. See **modulation**.

Key relationship

Keys with a similar number of sharps or flats to the 'home' key are regarded as near; those with a radically different number are distant. Thus F major, G major and A minor are all near keys for C major; D♭ major, F♯ major and G♯ minor are distant.

Key signature

Arrangement of accidentals at the beginning of a piece indicating the 'key' to the performer. There are 15 key signatures: seven **sharp**, seven **flat** and C major which has no **sharps** or **flats**.

A Major   B♭ Major

Kick drum

Another name for bass drum, so-called because it is played by the drummer's foot pressing down on a pedal.

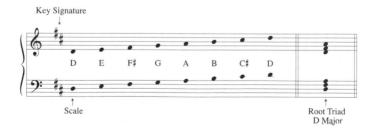

Key Signature

D E F♯ G A B C♯ D

Scale

Root Triad
D Major

Koto

Japanese zither-like instrument with a
rectangular body, usually 13 strings
tuned in various pentatonic scales. The
notes are fingered with the left hand,
struck by the right. The koto is part of
the traditional ensemble with the
shamisen and shakuhachi.

Krautrock

Unfortunate but persistent label for
certain types of rock emanating from
Germany in the 1970s. The term is
associated most with Can and
Kraftwerk, and therefore implies some
degree of experimentation and use of
synthesizers.

Largo
(I) Slow and stately.

Lead guitar
In pop and **rock** music the guitar (usually electric) that counterpoints the vocal **melody** and provides solos. Brought to prominence in the 1960s British **Blues** boom and by the first generation of **rock** guitar virtuosi - Eric Clapton, Jeff Beck, Jimmy Page, Jimi Hendrix, Carlos Santana, etc.

Leading note
The 7th note of the scale, in many scales a **semitone** away from the **octave**.

Leakage
In the studio, instruments are traditionally 'isolated' so that each microphone only picks up the instrument in front of it and not others playing nearby. High volumes, such as generated by rock bands, can cause leakage of one instrument into another instrument's microphone.

Legato
(I) To play smoothly.

Ledger line
Sometimes spelt 'ledger'. Small line added to facilitate the writing of a note above or below the **stave**.

Leitmotif
(G) 'leading motif'. The use of a repeated phrase or musical idea throughout a longer piece to symbolise a person, an object or an idea. Especially significant in the works of Wagner.

Leslie effect
Sound created by feeding a signal through a Leslie speaker revolving at high speed causing pitch fluctuations in the note. Most commonly used for keyboard and guitar. The **bridge** section of Cream's 'Badge' (1969) illustrates the sound of a guitar fed through a Leslie.

Libretto
The words for an opera or musical, originally printed as a small book for the audience to read during the performance.

Lick
Slang term used mostly in pop/rock music, to describe a short musical phrase which many be repeated often during the song.

Liturgy
The text of a Christian service set to music.

Locrian

One of the seven Greek **modes** or
scales, the Locrian mode is the **interval**
sequence B C D E F G A B (a natural
minor scale with a flattened 2nd and
5th).

Loop

Originally, a section of tape edited to
repeat a sound for the length of a
recording. In the 1960s The Beatles
experimented with tape loops, using
them to stunning effect on songs like
'Tomorrow Never Knows' and 'Being
For The Benefit Of Mr Kite'. Digital
technology has made looping an
effortless procedure, either by
programming or sampling.

Lullaby

A cradle-song.

Lute

Forerunner of the guitar, the lute was
popular throughout Europe during the
Middle Ages until the mid-C17th. The
number of strings and body dimensions
varied greatly, though common features
include catgut frets, strings doubled at
the same pitch, a curved-back body, and
ornately decorated sound-holes. In the
1590s player-composers such as John
Dowland developed a complex,
contrapuntal style for the instrument.

Lydian

One of the seven Greek **modes** or
scales, the Lydian mode is the **interval**
sequence F G A B C D E F (a **major
scale** with a raised 4th).

Lyric

(i) The words to a song.
(ii) Lyrical: to play in a melodious,
'singing' manner.

Madrigal

C16th unaccompanied piece, usually **contrapuntal** and secular in theme, to be sung by a small group of voices in a domestic setting.

Maestoso

(I) 'Majestically'.

Mainstream

Music generally agreed to be of a current trend.

Major interval

Two notes which are a tone, two tones, 2¹/₂, 3¹/₂, or 4¹/₂ tones apart defined in relation to the **major scale**.

Major scale

Pattern of notes arranged according to the **interval** sequence Tone-Tone-Semitone-Tone-Tone-Tone Semitone.

Measure

U.S. expression for a **bar**.

Mediant

The **third** note of the scale.

Medley

Practice of combining extracts from several songs or pieces into one continuous performance, sometimes with the object of enabling more popular tunes to be heard in the limited time of a concert.

Melisma

(i) A group of notes sung to one syllable.
(ii) Elaborate decoration of a **melody** by a singer intended to intensify the emotion but often merely showcasing the singer's technique. Typical of black music styles such as **soul**, **rhythm'n'blues** and **gospel**.

Melody

Sequence of single notes, either sung or played by an instrument, which are the focus of interest.

Melodic minor scale
Scale created when the sixth and 7th
notes of the natural minor scale are
raised and then restored to their normal
pitch coming down. The fixed melodic
minor raises these notes both ascending
and descending.

C minor

Natural

Mellotron
1960s keyboard designed to imitate
strings, flutes and other orchestral
instruments. Physically heavy and
subject to tuning problems, the
Mellotron has long since been
superseded by digital synthesisers, but
retains a reedy charm apparent on The
Beatles' 'Strawberry Fields Forever'
(1967) and The Moody Blues' 'Nights
In White Satin' (1968).

Metronome
Electronic or spring-operated device for
creating a regular rhythmic pulse at any
tempo, enabling the player to practise to
a steady beat.

Microtone
Pitch-**interval** smaller than a **semitone**.
Microtones are used in non-Western
musical traditions, some **rock** music,
and avant-garde **classical** music.

Middle C
Note at or near the middle of a piano's
range, written on the first ledger line
below the stave (treble clef). The
frequency of middle C at concert pitch
(where A=440Hz) is 261.52Hz (not
256Hz as is often stated for
mathematical convenience).

Middle Eight
Section of a song that comes after the
second **chorus** and acts as a **bridge** to
either a solo, a verse or another **chorus**.
Eight is a typical length but the term
applies regardless of the number of bars.

MIDI
Musical Instrument Digital Interface.
Revolutionary system by which digital
instruments can 'talk' to one another and
be linked for recording and live
performance.

Minim
Also known as a Half-note; a note
lasting two **crotchet** beats.

Minor interval
Interval of a **semitone**, $1^1/_2$ tones, 4 or 5 tones defined in relation to the **minor scale**.

minor 3rd   minor 6th

Minor scale
The minor scale has three main forms. In A the natural minor runs A B C D E F G A; the harmonic minor is A B C D E F G♯ A; the **melodic minor** A B C D E F♯ G♯ A with the two **sharps** removed when descending.

Minuet
Popular dance form of the C17th and C18th in triple time.

Mix
(Verb): final stage in the recording process, where combined parts in a multitrack recording are balanced and additional effects added. The multitrack is then copied to a stereo recording, resulting in *(noun)* a mix. At a concert, the mix is the balance of instruments coming through the P.A.

Mixolydian
One of the seven Greek **modes** or scales, the Mixolydian **mode** is the **interval** sequence G A B C D E F G (a **major scale** with a flattened 7th). Since **blues** music often flattens the 7th, this scale is common in pop / **rock** music,

the resulting straight major **chord** VII replacing the less useful **diminished** VII of the **major scale** proper.

G   A   B   C   D   E   F   G

M. O. R.
Acronym for 'Middle of the Road'. Mildly derogatory term for a highly commercial, smooth style of popular music typified by the 1970s American duo The Carpenters. See also **A.O.R.**

Mode
Scale originating in ancient Greece. There are 7 main modes: **Ionian**, **Dorian**, **Phrygian**, **Lydian**, **Mixolydian**, **Aeolian** and **Locrian**.

Moderato
(I) Played moderately.

Modulation
Key-change. Modulation is an essential feature of longer works to prevent monotony. Key-changes create significant contrasts of meaning and emotion, as the listener is moved from one tonal centre to another. Keys with a similar number of **sharps** or **flats** to the 'home' key are regarded as 'near'; those with a radically different number are 'distant'. Thus F major, G major and A minor are all near keys for C major; D♭ major, F♯ major and G♯ minor are distant.

Monitor
See **foldback**.

Motown
Short-hand for the popular **soul** music released on the Detroit Motown record label 1960-72. 'Classic' 1960s Motown was danceable, with a strong beat, sometimes four-to-the-bar snare drum, and highly commercial. Along with Atlantic and Stax, it was the most important label for black music in that period.

Multitrack
Type of recording (either on analogue tape or digital medium) in which musical parts are laid down side by side on a number of 'tracks'. During the first half of the 1960s multitrack recording was on 2, 3 or 4 track. The second half of the 1960s saw 8-track become the norm, quickly followed by 16, 24, 32 and 48 in the 1970s.

Musique concrete
Form of highbrow C20th experimental music concerned with creating collages of sound on tape.

Mute
Technique whereby the normal sound of an instrument is slightly damped or blocked, creating a different, less forceful sound. With a trumpet this is achieved by a hand-held plug which almost seals the hole; on the guitar muting is achieved by putting the side of the picking hand on the strings very

near the **bridge** or tailpiece.

Nashville tuning

Guitar tuning in which the lower four strings E A D G are replaced with thinner strings so that they can be tuned an **octave** higher than usual.

String no:	6th	5th	4th	3rd	2nd	1st
Note name:	E	A	D	G	B	E

Natural

Type of **accidental** which cancels out the effect of a **sharp** or **flat**.

B flat   B natural

New Age music

New Age music has its roots in Brian Eno's ambient experiments; it aims for a remedial effect, promising to soothe the nerves and uplift the spirit by inducing tranquil, reflective states. Synth voices and approximations of ethnic instruments such as pan-pipes blend with string sounds in washes of reverb. Rhythm or dissonance are reduced to a minimal role in favour of simplistic melodies and harmony. Typically, 'authentic' elements such as plainsong or folk melodies are combined with sophisticated electronica to create a contemplative and calming atmosphere.

New Romantic

Phase in popular music during the early 1980s typified by artists such as Soft Cell, Spandau Ballet, Duran Duran, The Human League, and Gary Numan. New Romantic music was typified by short, commercial songs and androgynous imagery but unlike glam rock rejected the hegemony of the guitar. Instead it embraced the new technology of early drum machines and synthesizers, with the consequence that much of it now sounds dated.

New Wave

New Wave was the second shock from the U.K. punk-rock explosion of 1976. It softened the political and anarchic aspects of punk, and made the songs more musical and therefore more commercial without relinquishing the no-nonsense get-to-the-point spirit. Unlike New Romantics, most New Wave was guitar oriented. Significant artists who surfed New Wave to success included Elvis Costello, Graham Parker, Television, The Police, Talking Heads and The Pretenders.

Nickleodeon

Early C20th mechanical device which generated music from a specially designed roll of paper on the insertion of a coin. Found in public places, these were superseded by the jukebox in the 1930s.

Ninth

The compound interval comprising an octave plus a (major, minor or augmented) second. A ninth **chord** is a second octave chord where the seventh and ninth are added to the basic triad.

Major 9th   C9

Nocturne

An instrumental piece of indeterminate form, usually with a dreamy night-time quality, popularised by the pianist / composer Chopin in the C19th.

Noise gate

Sound processing device which automatically silences ('gates') a channel when the incoming signal drops below a certain volume, thus preventing unwanted background noise.

Notation

Any method for writing music down on paper. Standard notation systems use the five-line **stave**. Some instruments such as the guitar have their own alternative which is used either alone or in conjunction with the traditional **stave**. See **tablature**.

Note-row

Term used in serial or twelve-tone music to describe a series of notes which are taken as the basis for an atonal composition – one not written according to traditional scales, keys or harmony.

Octave

The distance between any note and the same note 12 semitones higher or lower.

Octet

Composition for eight instruments.

Off-beat

In a bar of 4/4 the off-beat falls on the even-numbered eighth notes: 1 2 3 4 5 6 7 8. The odd-numbered notes carry the beat. The 2 and 4 quarter-note beats can also be treated in a similar fashion depending on tempo. Deliberate accenting of the off-beat is a hallmark of **reggae**.

Open score

The use of a separate **stave** for individual voices rather than combining onto one.

Open string

A string on an instrument such as the guitar or violin which is played without a finger on it. Open string notes have a different timbre - or sound quality - to fretted or fingered notes.

Open tuning

Guitar technique whereby standard EADGBE tuning is changed so that the open strings will produce a major or minor **chord**. DADF♯AD is open D, DGDGBD open G and EBEGBE open E minor. There are many altered tunings like DADGAD which go beyond a simple **triad**. Open tunings are popular with folk fingerstyle players and for **bottleneck** playing, and have been used in a **rock** context by guitarists such as Jimmy Page of Led Zeppelin and Keith Richards of the Rolling Stones.

Opera

Large scale work for **orchestra** and singers, featuring narrative and characters, with defined song sections (**arias**) and recitatives (where a lyric is sung on one note). Operas can be tragic or comic, serious or light-hearted.

Opus

Literally meaning 'work', name used in classical music to catalogue a composition, e.g. Beethoven's Thirty-three Variations on a Waltz by Diabelli in C for piano, Opus 120.

Oratorio

C18th extended work for voices and an ensemble often with a sacred theme.

Orchestra

Largest ensemble of instruments with all types represented - strings, brass, woodwind, keyboard and percussion - regarded as the most powerful combination in Western **classical** music.

Orchestration
The art of writing for an orchestra, or taking a piece first written for a solo instrument or small group and arranging it for an orchestra.

Ornaments
See **grace notes**.

Ostinato
(I) Lit. 'Persistent'. A musical figure constantly repeated, often in the **bass**.

Overtones
Higher parts of a note distinguished from the **fundamental**.

Overture
Piece of music originally intended as the introduction to a longer work but sometimes becoming popular enough to be played in its own right.

P

P. A.

Abbrev. for 'public address' A sound system designed to amplify the voice or a small group of musicians. In a **rock** band microphones are usually placed in front of the **backline** amplifiers and then re-amplified by the P. A.

Pad

Recording term used to mean providing an unobtrusive chordal backdrop of some kind (often on a synth) behind the main lead instrument or voice.

Pan

To move a musical signal to the left or right of a stereo image during a mix. Late 1960s pop-rock records often used panning to give the music a pictorial quality, as can be heard on the **coda** of Jimi Hendrix's 'House Burning Down' (Electric Ladyland, 1968).

Parallel motion

Where musical parts move together in direction, as in Gregorian chant's consecutive **perfect fifths**.

Passing-note

A note which by itself produces a momentary discord but which serves to connect two chord notes.

Pedal point

A note repeated in the **bass** part while **chords** change and move above it. When this **bass** note is the key-note it is called a tonic pedal.

Pentatonic

A five note scale often associated with oriental music. Much **lead guitar** soloing in **rock** and **blues** uses either the pentatonic minor (in A, A C D E G) or the pentatonic major (in A, A B C♯ E F♯).

Major, in A

minor, in A

Perfect cadence

A **chord** change from V to I at the end of a phrase, used to finish or establish a new key. The modulatory effect of a perfect cadence is strengthened if the V **chord** is turned into a **dominant** 7th.

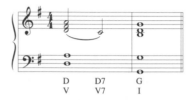

D	D7	G
V	V7	I

Perfect Fifth

Interval of 3 1/2 tones naturally occurring between the 1st and 5th notes of a major or minor scale.

D Major   G Major

Perfect Fourth

Interval of 2 1/2 tones naturally occurring between the 1st and 4th note of a major or minor scale.

D Major   G Major

Phrasing

The art of grouping and interpreting notes in performance to give them expression.

Phrygian

One of the seven Greek **modes** or scales, the Phrygian **mode** is the **interval** sequence E F G A B C D E (the natural minor scale with a flattened 2nd).

E F G A B C D E

Piano

(I) Volume direction meaning soft or softly.

Piano reduction

The condensing of music originally written for an ensemble onto a single piano part.

Pickup

Device for electrically amplifying the sound of an **acoustic** instrument. See **humbucker**.

Pizzicato

(I) Abbrev. pizz. Technique used by string players in which the string is plucked rather than bowed, creating a more percussive, but less sustained sound.

Plagal cadence

The **chord** movement IV to I at the end of a phrase.

IV	I
F	C

Plainsong

Type of sacred vocal music dating back a thousand years in Europe, sung in free **rhythm** from a four-line **stave**.

Plectrum

Also known as a pick, small piece of plastic used to strike the string of a guitar or mandolin. Plectrums come in many shapes, sizes and thicknesses.

Pocket symphony

Informal term associated with American songwriter Brian Wilson, describing his increasingly ambitious vision, in the 1960s, of the pop song as a masterpiece of invention in miniature. Initially influenced by Phil Spector's wall of sound, this approach bore fruit on The Beach Boys' '*Pet Sounds*' and 'Good Vibrations' (1966).

Polyphony

Literally many voices, thus in music a piece in which there are interweaving melodies.

Portamento

(I) See **slur** and **glissando**.

Power-chord

(Colloq.) **Rock** term for a **perfect fifth**, with the root note and sometimes the fifth also doubled at a higher **octave**. Distorted fifths are crucial to the rhythm parts of heavier **rock** styles.

Pre-amp

Effects unit designed to boost the original signal.

Presto

(I) 'Quickly' (**tempo** indication).

Progressive rock

Once a term of approval but now often derogatory. Musical movement of the 1970s involving emphasis on virtuosity, increasing ambition and experimentation in the studio, a move away from the three minute 4/4 song, and lyrics that tried to go beyond pop's perennial boy-meets-girl themes. Attempts to mimic or borrow the forms of **classical** music (the creation of **rock** concertos and operas) revealed progressive rock's desire to satisfy the counter-culture's desire for its own 'high art'. Definitive prog-rock albums include *The Lamb Lies Down On Broadway* (Genesis, 1974), *Tales From Topographic Oceans* (Yes, 1974), and *Dark Side Of The Moon* (Pink Floyd, 1973).

Punk rock

Rock style characterised by brevity
(songs were rarely longer than a few
minutes), harmonic simplicity, fast
tempos, aggressive delivery and
sneering pitch-indifferent vocals. The
U.S. punk scene developed on the East
coast in the early 1970s; UK punk came
to prominence in late 1975-1977,
overthrowing the old progressive
musical order. Definitive punk rock
albums include *Never Mind The
Bollocks* (Sex Pistols, 1977), *London
Calling* (The Clash, 1979) and *The
Ramones* (The Ramones, 1976).

Q

Quadruple time
Another name for **common time**; four beats in a **bar**.

Quadruplet
Four notes played in the time it would normally take to play three of the same value. The quadruplet is to compound time what the triplet is to simple time.

Quantization
Technique of MIDI sequencing and electronic drum machines that automatically corrects slight deviances in timing thus producing a part that is perfectly in time.

Quartal harmony
A type of harmony where chord construction is based on the interval of a fourth rather than a third.

Quarter-tone
See **microtone**.

Quaver
Note which is an eighth of a beat, and half the length of a **crotchet**, or whole note. A **semiquaver** is half again, making it sixteenth of a beat.

Quintuple time
Five beats in a **bar**. The asymmetry of 5/4 is striking, especially in popular music. Dave Brubeck's *'Take Five'* (1960) is a typical example.

R

Raga

Indian music form involving scale-like figures which are taken as the basis for improvisation. Ragas have established associations in terms of their mood or the time when they are suitable to be performed.

Ragtime

Type of popular music from the early C20th immortalised by the piano instrumentals of Scott Joplin and an allusion in T. S. Eliot's poem *The Waste Land* (1922). Ragtime is marked by an inventive, almost comic **syncopation**. It was eventually subsumed into early **jazz**.

Rallentando

(I) Direction to slow down gradually. *Abbrev.* rall.

Rap

Musical style originating in the Afro-American community popular in the late 1980s and 1990s. **Melody** is replaced by a highly rhythmic delivery of rhymed, colloquial lyrics over a basic beat, often sampled. Influential artists include Public Enemy, Beastie Boys and De La Soul.

Rasguedo

Picking-hand technique used by **flamenco** guitarists involving explosive sequential uncurling of the fingers to strike the strings.

Real time

A term coined in the wake of the digital music revolution, to describe a non-programmed musical performance recorded at the same speed as the intended playback speed.

Recapitulation

Generally, to re-state an earlier musical theme. More precisely this covers the third part of **sonata** form where the initial thematic material returns in the tonic key.

Recitative

Device used in an opera to communicate a lyric passage which is not suited to being harmonised in an elaborate manner. The words attempt to approximate the rhythms of speech and are chanted on one note.

Refrain

A repeated passage in a song equivalent to a **chorus**. In folk-song a line or lines that comes at the end of each verse.

Reggae

Jamaican popular music which developed in the 1960s and gained an international audience through the success of Bob Marley and The Wailers in the 1970s. Reggae is typified by electric instrumentation, simple harmonic changes (I-II is a favourite) and above all by its constant emphasis of the off-beat and short phrases on the electric bass which have distinct pauses between them. Other variants include Dub, where a piece is lengthened and subjected to extensive re-mixing including the foregrounding of the bass and the abrupt insertion of multi-tap echo. Lyrically, some reggae has strong links with Rastafarianism.

Related keys
See **Modulation**.

Relative keys
Major and minor keys which share the same key-signature, but with one accidental raising the 7th degree of the minor scale. The relative minor is **chord** VI of the major key and is always a minor 3rd (three semitones) below the major key note. Eg:

| G major | relative minor | E minor |
| F# | key signature | F# + D# |

Resolution
General term for the release of a tension in music caused by a **dissonance** of some kind changing to a **consonance**.

Rest
Symbol used to indicate a period of silence in a **bar**. There are individual symbols for each equivalent note. Adding a dot after a rest increases its length by ½.

quaver rest = ½ beat   dotted crotchet rest = 1 ½ beats

Reverb
Short for reverberation, the natural **acoustic** property of a space, characterised by a number of factors such as the length of echo. Reverb is an essential effect in the recording process, added at the mixing stage to give 'life' to a recording. Different periods of popular music have favoured different types of reverb, the 1980s, for example, using large amounts of reverb on drums. The 1990s have tended to favour a **'drier'** sound.

Rhapsody
A medium-length instrumental piece of no set form often for piano with a romantic or fantastic character. In popular music Gershwin's 'Rhapsody In Blue' and Queen's 'Bohemian Rhapsody' offer two highly contrasted examples.

Rhythm

One of the three foundations of most Western music, along with **melody** and **harmony**. Rhythm comprises the **tempo** of music, the type of beat, the number of beats in a **bar**, and the rhythm patterns generated by different instruments and melodic lines.

Rhythm and Blues (R'n'B)

Post-war Afro-American popular music having some gospel elements but also arising from the electrification of rural **blues** in cities like Chicago. As its name suggests, R'n'B has an emphatic **rhythm** and a tough, earthy quality, and is more of an ensemble style. It influenced rock'n'roll in the 1950s and groups like The Beatles, The Rolling Stones and The Who incorporated something of its feel in their early music. R'n'B itself persisted as a musical category through the 1960s despite yielding some of its territory to the smoother genre of '**soul**'. Now also used to describe some modern soul and dance music.

Riff

(Colloq.) A short musical phrase of about 2 bars, which is the focus of interest in a piece of music, with any vocal **melody** that may be present. Riffs are essential to **rock** music, where they are played on the guitar. Deep Purple's 'Smoke On The Water' (1972), Cream's 'Sunshine Of Your Love' (1967) and Dire Straits' 'Money For Nothing' (1985) are all riff-driven songs.

Risoluto

(I) Played in a resolute or bold manner.

Ritenuto

(I) Lit. 'held back'. Indication to play slower. Not a gradual slowing of **tempo** as indicated by rallentando.

Rock

Popular music form developed from a mixture of country, **blues** and **rhythm'n'blues**, exemplified first in the 1950s by the rock'n'roll songs of Elvis Presley, Little Richard, Chuck Berry et al, in the 1960s by The Beatles, The Rolling Stones, The Who and many others. Rock has in common with pop a grounding in the three or four minute song, with extensive repetition, a relatively simple harmonic vocabulary, and a fierce marking of the 4/4 beat. It differs from pop in being more aggressive, and lyrically and musically more experimental and adventurous. Pop has always been indifferent to being judged ephemeral; rock has often aspired to be taken seriously by 'high' culture.

Rockabilly

Type of 1950s American popular music which is closely related to rock'n'roll but places a stronger emphasis on the country elements in it. This is reflected in the choice of instruments, such as acoustic guitars and double bass. The energy and good-time feel of rockabilly made it popular for dancing.

Romanticism

A term used correctly in contrast to **classical** to describe the main trend of European music in the period 1790-1900. Romanticism saw both the composer and the **virtuoso** performer elevated to almost god-like status. Romantic music is concerned first and foremost with evoking emotion, hence it is dramatic, lyrical, dreamy, turbulent, and pushed beyond the forms and tonal rules of the C18th in order to achieve these effects. The outcome was the undermining of traditional tonality by composers like Wagner and Debussy.

Rondo

Compositional form in which an initial section in the tonic key is followed by a contrasting section, then the first section, then a third section, in the pattern ABACAD etc.

Root position

Chord in which the root note is the lowest. See **inversion**.

Round

Music for several voices in which after the first voice has completed its melodic phrase, the second voice begins with the same phrase, followed by a third and fourth while the first and second voices take up their next phrases.

Rubato

Expressive device by which the performer ignores the strict time of a piece, introducing pronounced pauses. Often used when playing C19th romantic music such as Chopin's Nocturnes.

S

Sampling

Electronic device popularised in the mid-1980s enabling the copying of a few seconds of sound which can then be manipulated on a **MIDI** synth or computer **sequencer**.

Sarabande

Instrumental dance popular in the C16th, in its later form becoming the third movement of a **Suite**.

Scale

Linear arrangement of notes, usually spanning one **octave**, from which the sense of **key** and **harmony** can be derived. Main forms include **major**, **minor**, **whole tone**, and **mode**.

Scat singing

Singing technique involving the improvisation of a tune, as though the voice were an instrument. To facilitate this, nonsense syllables - often alliterative - are used. Scat singing is a recognised jazz technique.

Second

Interval of 1 semitone (minor second, C-Db), 1 tone (major second, C-D) or 3 semitones (augmented second, C-D#).

Major 2nd   Minor 2nd Augmented 2nd

Semi-acoustic

Type of hollow-body electric guitar fitted with pick-ups but able to produce some acoustic sound. Semi-acoustics have traditionally been popular with jazz players, in contrast to rock players who favour the solid-body electric.

Semibreve

Whole note, lasting for four beats of a 4/4 bar. A breve lasted four **minim** beats of 4/2 but is very rare in modern music.

1 - 2 - 3 - 4   1 - 2 - 3 - 4

Semiquaver

See **quaver**.

Semitone

Half of a **tone**: there are 12 in an **octave**.

Sequencer

Type of computer software which allows a piece of music to be programmed, edited, recorded and played back automatically. Information goes to the computer, usually from a **MIDI** keyboard, but can also be entered and changed via the computer keyboard. Sequencing is to music what word-processing is to writing. Sequencers are phrase-based, pattern-based or linear.

Serenade

C18th instrumental piece designed to be played in the later evening. Modern connotation is of a gentle, lilting, romantic piece

Seventh

Can refer to the **leading note** of a scale, or a chord. There are three main types of seventh **chord**: the **dominant** seventh (C E G B♭), the major seventh (C E G B) and the minor seventh (C E♭ G B♭)

Major 7th   C7   Cmin7

Sharp

Accidental, indicating the raising of a note by a **semitone**.

Sight-reading

The ability to sing or play a piece of music printed in traditional **notation** without ever having seen it before. Many musical examinations require demonstration of some ability to sight-read.

Simple time

Type of **rhythm** where the beat is always divisible by an even number. See also **duple** and **compound** time.

Sitar

Stringed instrument central to Indian music developed over a number of centuries, attaining its modern form in the last century. The sitar has a long neck and a small bowl-like body. The strings are not pressed against a fretboard (as with a guitar) but held down behind frets which are metal hoops. These curved frets enable the pitch of any given note to be raised almost an **octave** by simply pulling the string downwards. A set of secondary strings provide **drone** effects. The sitar is played with a small piece of wire fitted on the end of the finger. Western awareness of the sitar is mostly due to The Beatles' recordings and the concerts of Ravi Shankar.

Skiffle

Originally a black music form of the 1930s, skiffle was revived in poverty-struck post-war Britain by white teenagers in the 1950s. Skiffle was an energetic, three or four **chord** song form, played on unamplified instruments like **acoustic** guitar, harmonica, tea-chest bass, etc. It arose in the brief musical lull between the end of 1950s rock'n'roll and the tidal wave of beat music inspired by The Beatles. Its most famous exponent in the U. K. was Lonnie Donegan.

Slapback

A type of echo devised in the 1950s and heard on many of the early Sun recordings of Elvis Presley. The echo is a single repeat coming shortly after the original note.

Slide

Guitar technique. A **slur** from one note to another where the first is struck but the second is created simply by the movement of the finger. Also see **bottleneck**.

Slur

Technique where a player moves from one note to another by a smooth ascent or descent of pitch.

Snare

Part of the standard drum kit, the snare has a metal or wooden circular frame with a taut skin stretched across the top, and a set of metal wires underneath which vibrate when the skin is struck. The snare is the loudest, easiest-heard part of the kit and in popular music is responsible for driving the beat.

Sonata

Structure used for the first movement of a symphony and **concertos**. The sonata form is characterised by a First Subject, a Bridge section which changes **key** to the **dominant**, the **key** of the next theme - the Second Subject. These in total form the **Exposition**. After a double bar-line the music moves to the Development and eventually the **Recapitulation** using the First and Second Subjects.

Song cycle

A form devised by Schubert in the C19th where a number of songs could be linked to make a larger work.

Soprano

The highest span for the female voice, roughly from **middle C** to the second G above it.

Soul music

The term now covers many different styles of predominantly commercial Afro-American music. It originated in the 1960s, when elements of R'n'B, **blues**, and gospel were combined with a pop sensibility. The resulting mix, typified by much of the output of black artists on the **Motown**, Atlantic and Stax labels, was highly danceable yet with a stronger sense of **melody** and song structure than later dance music of the 1970s, 80s and 90s. Soul music is characterised by syncopated rhythms, a **harmony** that makes frequent use of minor 7 / major 7 **chords**, and a declamatory, passionate vocal style.

Soundcheck

Run-through before a live concert to test equipment is functioning and to enable the sound engineers to get a good mix.

Staccato

Type of note (with a dot above or underneath it) in which the duration of the note is shortened.

Standard tuning

Guitar term for the usual tuning of E A D G B E in contrast to altered or **open tuning**.

Stave

Arrangement of five lines on which music is traditionally written. The type of **clef** used will determine which pitches a given stave covers.

Stepwise Motion

A type of musical progression by **tone** or **semitone** increments.

Strat

Shortened form of Stratocaster, Leo Fender's world-famous 1950s electric guitar design. The Strat is characterised by three single-coil pickups, a five-way selector switch and a tremolo arm. The so-called 'superstrat' of the 1980s was an attempt by other companies to update the Strat design.

String Quartet

Ensemble consisting of four stringed instruments - first and second violin, viola and cello.

Subdominant

The fourth note and **chord** of the scale.

Subdominant (F)
Chord of F

Submediant

The sixth note and **chord** of the scale.

Submediant (A)
Chord of Am

Suite

A group of dances, originally in the classical suite in a single **key** and constructed in **binary form**. Although a range of dances could be featured, the staple forms were the **Allemande**, Courante, Gigue, **Minuet** and **Sarabande**.

Supertonic

The second note and **chord** of the scale.

Supertonic (D)
Chord of Dm

Suspension

Harmonic effect where tension is created and then resolved. The most common type is the suspended fourth and suspended second **chords**. In the first, C F G becomes C E G; in the second, C D G becomes C E G. On both instances the **third** is suspended, thus rendering the chord neither major nor minor.

Sus4   Sus2

synthesis greatly improved the authenticity of the synth's imitations of orchestral instruments.

Swing feel
Rhythmic approach used in **blues** and **jazz** where the quavers of simple 4/4 are played more as if they were the quaver/crotchet combination of 12/8.

Sympathetic resonance
The ability of a string on an instrument to generate tones from other strings on the same instrument by vibrations travelling through its body. This is an important part of the colouration of the tone. Thus when the top E string on the guitar is played, part of the sound then heard depends on the bottom E (two octaves lower) vibrating 'in sympathy'.

Symphony
A large-scale work in four movements for **orchestra**.

Syncopation
Rhythmic effect created by playing on the off-beat.

Synthesizer
Electronic keyboard developed in the 1960s capable of generating different sounds and wave-forms. The earliest were monophonic - only able to produce a single note at a time - but polyphonic synths soon became the norm. Digital

T

Tabla

Small Indian hand-drum, tuned to different pitches, somewhat similar to bongos but with their own distinctive sound. Used to accompany the **sitar**.

Tablature

Alternate method of notating guitar music where six lines represent the six strings and the fret-number of each note is written on the appropriate line. Early tablature such as that used for the lute in Elizabethan England also gave rhythmic indications.

Open strings of the guitar:

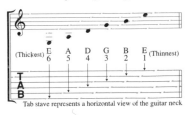

Tab stave represents a horizontal view of the guitar neck

Example of notation and TAB

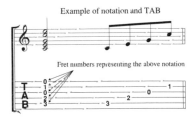

Fret numbers representing the above notation

Tapping

Technique popularised by U.S. electric guitarist Eddie Van Halen in the late 1970s, endemic in 1980s heavy rock, further developed by Steve Vai and Joe Satriani. The fretboard is struck with the fingers of the picking hand, generating fast **arpeggio** figures.

Techno

Type of popular music of the 1990s largely composed in the digital domain with **sequencers**, computers, samplers and drum machines, characterised by rapid **tempos**, an extremely simple **harmony**, sound effects, and an ethos which makes a virtue of the 'mechanical' impression such equipment easily produces.

Temperament

Most modern instruments use a system of tuning called '**equal temperament**' in which the **octave** is divided into twelve equal semitones all of which are slightly out of tune. Earlier systems included 'just' temperament which by making the **third** and fifth perfect created **chords** I, IV and V which were in tune.

Tempo

The speed of a piece of music. E.g:
[♩] = 120 bpm (beats per minute).

Tenor

Male voice part spanning from D in the centre of the bass clef to the first G on the treble **stave**.

Tenuto

(I) Lit. 'held'. Opposite to **staccato**, notes are held for their full length and sometimes even slightly extended.

Ternary

As **binary** form consists of two sections, ternary form consists of three: a first musical idea (section A) succeeded by a section B, and then section A repeated.

Tetrachord

Four notes separated by a tone, a tone, a tone and a semitone (C D E F). The **major scale** consists of two tetrachords.

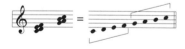

Theremin

Electronic device devised in the 1930s which looks like a radio aerial and creates a field around it sensitive to movement. The player moves a hand within this field and the Theremin translates this into pitch. Used by The Beach Boys on 'Good Vibrations' (1966), various early 1960s TV themes, in concert by Jimmy Page of Led Zeppelin in the 1970s, and has enjoyed a revival of interest in the 1990s.

Third

Interval of either a major third (C-E, two tones) or a minor third (C-E♭, 1¹/₂ tones). Also the third note of the **scale** and the middle note of a simple **triad** (C E G, C E♭ G).

Major 3rd   minor 3rd

Threshold

The level at which a sound processing effect switches on. A control marked 'threshold' is often seen on studio equipment such as compressors, noise gates and enhancers.

Tie

Line connecting two notes adding the duration of the second to the first. Only the first is played.

Tierce de Picardie

(F) **Cadence** at the end of a minor **key** piece which causes the music to end in the minor's tonic major. Such a **cadence** in G minor would end on G major.

V - I

Tierce de Picardie

V - I

Timbre

The tonal quality of a voice or instrument.

Time code

Form of digital data used in recording which can be used to lock other instruments to play along with what has already been recorded.

Time signature

Two numbers at the beginning of a piece of music indicating the number of beats in a bar and the type of beat.

3 (crotchet) beats   6 quavers
in a bar   in a bar

Toccata

(Lit.) 'Touch-piece'. A C17th piece for keyboard, exhibiting florid **scale** work and **broken chord** accompaniment. Often linked with the **fugue**.

Tone

(i) **Interval** of 2 **semitones**, or between a pair of adjacent white notes on the piano (except E-F and B-C).
(ii) **Timbre** of an instrument or voice.

Tone poem

Also known as a symphonic poem, this is a one movement piece for **orchestra** intended to be in some way descriptive or narrative.

Tonic chord

Chord I of a **key**.

Tonic minor

Minor **key** which shares the same keynote as a major **key**. C minor is thus the tonic minor of C major (in contrast to the relative minor).

Transposition

The shifting of a piece of music from one **key** to another, sometimes to fit a vocalist's range. Also used as a compositional device, whereby a music phrase is repeated through different **keys**.

Transposing instruments

These instruments have their music written at a different pitch from the sound that they produce. Transposing instruments include most brass instruments and some of the woodwind. The E♭ saxophone, for example, sounds a major 6th lower than written.

E♭ alto saxophone sounds a major sixth below the written pitch. Rule: **Written C sounds E♭**

French Horn

Saxophone

Tremolando
(I) A technique involving the rapid re-striking of a note for its duration, rather than hitting the note once. Often used in string writing when the music requires a sense of drama and tension.

Tremolo
Musical effect produced by rapid variation in volume. cf. **vibrato**.

Tremolo arm
Device on an electric guitar attached to the tail-piece, allowing the strings to become movable and the player to slacken or raise the string-tension. Mild use creates the gentle **vibrato** heard on early 1960s recordings by The Shadows, more violent use creates spectacular glissandos, as can be heard vividly in Jimi Hendrix's performance of 'The Star-Spangled Banner' at Woodstock in August 1969.

Triad
A three note **chord**.

Trio
In jazz, a popular three-musician ensemble, usually comprising drums, piano and double bass. In rock, the 'power-trio' comprises drums, electric bass and electric guitar. The 'power' epithet has come to be applied because such rock trios tend to play at high volume levels to mask the absence of a harmony instrument if the guitar is soloing.

Triplet

Three equal notes played in the time of
two. Approximates the skipping **rhythm**
of compound time when in a **simple
time**.

Tritone

The **interval** of three tones (e.g. C-F♯)
known as the 'forbidden' or 'devil's'
interval of medieval church music. Its
dark discordant tone is essential to much
1980s **heavy metal**.

Truss rod

Metal rod that runs through the neck of
steel-strung guitars allowing
adjustments that can correct warping
and other similar distortions which may
set in over time.

Twelve-bar blues

Common form for **blues** and blues-
derived music such as rock'n'roll.
Chord I occupies bars 1-4, **chord** IV
bars 5-6, **chord** I bars 7-8, and the last
four bars are V, IV, I, V. This is usually
in a major **key** but minor **key blues** also
use this structure. There are many slight
variants, such as the 'quick-change'
blues where bar 2 is **chord** IV.

Twelve-note music

Atonal system devised by Schoenberg in
the early C20th, replacing keys and
scales with a twelve note series which is
then developed by the composer
throughout a piece.

Twin-neck

Type of guitar, usually electric, which
has two necks attached to the body. The
most popular configuration is a six-
string with a 12-string, typified by the
Gibson ES1275D, associated with
Jimmy Page of Led Zeppelin and John
McLaughlin of the Mahavishnu
Orchestra. Often dismissed as symbols
of rock pretension, these instruments do
in fact offer significant musical
potentials. The player may in the space
of a single song contrast 6 string with
12 string sounds, or use two different
tunings. These instruments also offer
some stunning possibilities with
sympathetic resonance.

Up beat
The unstressed beat that comes just before the bar line (in contrast to the down beat, the first of the next bar).

Ukelele
Small, short-necked instrument, originally related to the four-string Hawaiian guitar, popularised in the 1930s by the ukelele-banjo songs of George Formby Jnr.

Una corda
Direction to a pianist to depress the left, soft pedal, causing the hammers to only strike one string per note instead of three. The direction is ended with 'tre corda'.

Unequal voices
Somewhat anachronistic term for a vocal piece using male and female, i.e. mixed voices.

Unessential note
A note which is not part of the essential harmony, but is instead a passing or grace note.

Unison
Two notes of the same pitch.

Unison bend
Electric guitar technique for thickening phrases in **lead guitar** solos where two notes of the same pitch are generated. One is fretted, the other - usually a tone lower on the next string down - is bent to the required pitch.

V

Valve amp

Type of amplifier for electric instruments such as the guitar, utilising mid C20th vacuum-tube technology. The classic distortion of the rock guitar arose through guitarists over-stressing the valves in their amplifiers by playing at the highest volume the amp would permit. Valve amps are defined in contrast to solid-state transistor amps and, since the 1990s, digital amps.

Vamp

Verb and noun describing a simple chordal accompaniment to a song, originally consisting of triads in the left hand of a piano part, often extemporised from a chord sheet.

Variation

Compositional framework in which a theme is stated and then re-stated with varied harmony and arrangement. Elgar's Enigma Variations is a famous example.

Verse

Important part of popular songs, along with Chorus and Middle Eight. If the verse lays out the lyrical problem or situation, the Chorus supplies an answer or a response.

Vibrato

Musical effect produced by rapid variation in pitch. cf. **tremolo**

Viol

Early bowed string instrument popular in the C16th and C17th, ancestor of the modern violin family.

Violin

Small-bodied bowed instrument central to the orchestra, chiefly with a melodic function, tuned in fifths: G D A E.

Viola

Slightly deeper-toned version of the violin, tuned a fifth lower: C G D A. The orchestra's string section comprises viola with violin, cello and double bass.

Virtuoso

Anyone who has achieved a high degree of technical proficiency on an instrument.

Voicing

The choice of notes for a given chord. A simple triad has three notes but these can be played at many different pitches. These possibilities are each known as a voicing.

W

Wah-Wah

Foot-operated effect pedal which is connected in between the guitar and amplifier, altering the tone of a note to give a distinctly vocal effect. See Isaac Hayes' 'Theme From Shaft' (1971), the work of Melvin 'Wah-wah Watson' Ragin on many 60's Motown recordings, and Jimi Hendrix's intro to 'Voodoo Chile (Slight Return)' (1968) for some of the most famous uses of this gadget.

Walking bass

Bass style found in jazz and some rock'n'roll, which involves smooth, scale-like movement in eighth or quarter-notes.

Wall of sound

Phrase associated with 1960s record producer Phil Spector, describing his approach to arranging pop songs, which involved filling the studio with an enormous number of musicians, thus greatly increasing the number of parts, the frequency range and the various colours in the final mix.

Waltz

Popular C19th dance form in 3/4 time.

West Coast jazz

Style of restrained, improvisational jazz played by small ensemble, associated with California in the 1950s, and with performers such as Chet Baker and Dave Brubeck.

West Coast rock

Term describing a style of rock music played by US groups associated with California, San Francisco, etc. Its hey-day ran from about 1966-75. It often features harmony vocals and a free-spirited, breezy, open feel. Influential groups might include The Byrds, Jefferson Airplane, Love, The Grateful Dead, Spirit, mid-70s Fleetwood Mac and The Eagles.

Wet

Adjective to describe the percentage of a signal which has been altered by a sound effect such as **reverb**, in contrast to the 'dry' unaltered signal. During the mixing process decisions are made about the blending of wet and **dry** signal.

White noise

Sound comprised of random electrically-generated frequencies fused together into a 'fuzzy' static.

White note

On the piano the white notes are C D E F G A B (in contrast to the black keys which are **sharps** and **flats**).

Whole-tone scale

A **scale** consisting of six notes progressing in tones extending over an **octave**. For example, starting on C: C D E F♯ G♯ A♯ C.

- tone - tone - tone - tone - tone - tone -

Wolf note

A note rendered weaker than it should be by the **acoustic** idiosyncrasies of an instrument.

Word painting

Composition technique in Elizabethan madrigals where the movement or behaviour of a vocal line enacts the sense of the words. The word 'ascend' would have a rising melody; the word 'descend' a falling melody.

Xylophone

Percussion instrument consisting of bars of wood of different lengths to give different pitches, the top surface of each being slightly rounded. These are laid on a wooden frame and struck with small wooden hammers with rounded heads, creating a distinctive tonal but percussive sound.

Yodel

Singing technique associated with Alpine folk-song which involves extremely rapid fluctuations between a normal voice and falsetto.

Zither

A stringed instrument of the psaltery group, normally tuned A A D G C or A D G G C, designed to provide a single line melody with chordal accompaniment.

Index

Index